LEGAL HISTORY OF NEPAL

STRAIGHT OUTTA INSCRIPTIONS

AUPSON POKHREL

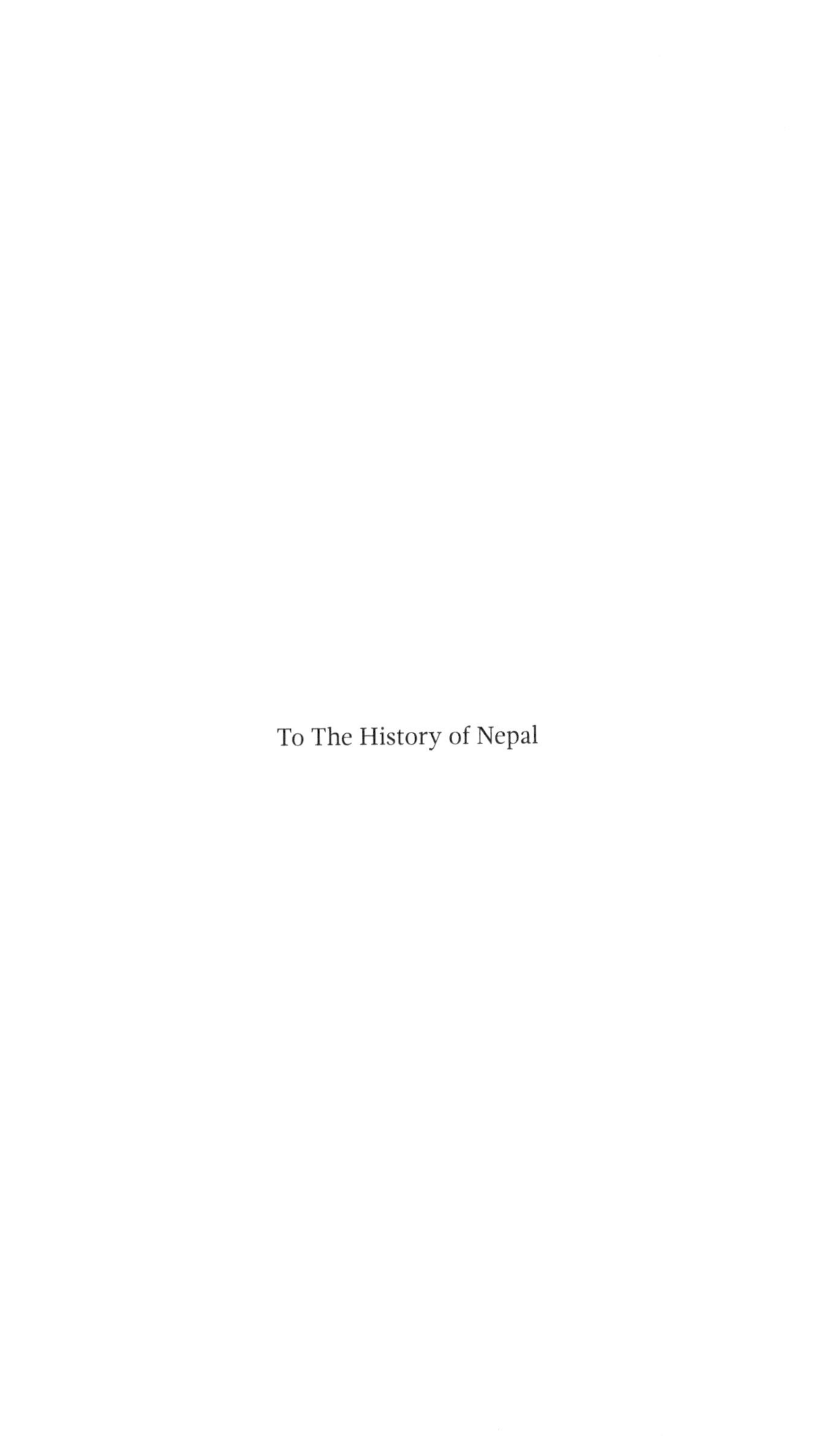

To The History of Nepal

Contents

Preface

Legal History of Nepal: Straight Outta Inscriptions covers the fundamental aspect of Nepalese Legal History. In fact, Nepalese History has been so much misrepresented through Interpretation that I have just stated what is needed to be stated. The Historical Progress of Administration and Legal System in each of these Period is stated with eloquency in my Opinion. Although Much Content of Modern Legal History has been left out, consciously, The Important Bits and Aspects of Legal History of Nepal has been covered. This Book shall act as an Introductory Discussion and Knowledege of Legal, Administrative and Constitutional History of Nepal. Thank You !

CHAPTER I

Gopal and Mahispal Dynasty

Introduction

Gopal Dynasty is the First Known Dynasty to rule Nepal. They were simply cow herders who migrated to the Kathmandu Valley. Gopal's started to settle in the valley, which was so moist for vegetation, so rich and dense in forests, with the presence of rivers and natural resources. Thus, they had a dense community in Kathmandu Valley

Kingship

According to Gopal Raja Bansawali, Gopal's became King of Nepal due to a cow named Brahuhri. Brahuhri went to a holy site and offered her milk at that site. It was a daily routine for her to go near the Bagmati River and offer her milk. Once the Gopal community found out about it, the head of the community, or Sardar excavated the place and found the "Jyotirlinga of Pashupatinath." Unfortunately, the Sardar was killed.

At that time, there existed a great saint by the name of "Ne" or simply Ne Muni. He was blessed to be the protector of that land. When he heard of the incident, he took it as a sign and made the son of the Sardar, King of Nepal. The Son of Sardar was Bhumi Gupta. So, he is known as the First King of Gopal Dynasty. They governed in a place called

Mata Tirtha, situated 4 miles southwest of Kathmandu.

Chronology

The Gopala dynasty was clever, or even wise, in that they claimed to be descended from the moon, or Lunar, i.e., Chandravanshi. They built great fables, from the myth of Krishna and Danasura to the alleged story of Ne Muni.

The following is a chronology of Gopala Dynasty rulers in Nepal (521 Years 7 Kings):

Bhumi Gupta, 86 years
Jaya Gupta, 73.5 years
Dharma Gupta, 91 years old
Harsha Gupta, 67 years
Bhim Gupta, 34 years
Mani Gupta, 37 years
Bishnu Gupta, 46 years
Jit Gupta, 71 years old, or Yaksha Gupta

Legacy and Evidences

Some of the Evidences for the Existence of Gopal Dynasty is:

1. The Chronology written during the reign of Jayastithi Malla named Gopal Raj

Bansawali (History of Kings) consists the name of Gopal's as the First Kings.

1. The Jyotirlinga of Pashupatinath, who is known to this day was discovered at the time.

2. Kathmandu Valley had long dried and very fertile for Animal Husbandry and Agriculture. Hence, it is obvious for any Dynasty to start ruling Nepal.
3. They inhabited in places such as Balambu, Kirtipur, Thankot etc. which exists to this day.
4. The Chronicles of William Kirkpatrick, Daniel Wright and Gopalraja Bansawali all contains Gopal Dynasty. So, it is accumulative proof of their existence.
5. Although the Myths were made to Justify Gopal Dynasty, the Myths have Geographical and Political Relevance such as Krishna cutting the gorge of Chovar etc.

Mahispal Dynasty

Introduction

Mahispal means buffalo herders. Although some historians refer to them as the "Abhir Mahispal Dynasty," Generally, the name Mahispal is used. Mahispal's were descendants of Abhir Dynasty. Hence, they are also called Abhir Mahispal.

Kingship

1. Bhasa Bansawali states that Yaksha Gupta became a Buddhist and neglected duties towards the crown. So, Bar Singh was called to rule of Nepal.
2. Mahispal's replaced Gopal Dynasty through War.
3. Jit Gupta (Last Gopal King) was childless. Hence, to ensure a ruler in the state Bar Singh was called to rule

over Nepal.

Chronology

The Chronology of the Kings of Mahispal Dynasty are:

1. Bar Singh: 49 Years
2. Jaya Singh: 71 Years 6 months
3. Bhuwan Singh: 41 Years

Mahispal Dynasty had three Kings and ruled Nepal for 161 years.

Another Chronology according to Bhasa Bansawali states 3 Kings of Mahispal Dynasty ruled for 111 years:

1. Bar Singh: 49 years
2. Jaya Mati Singh: 21 years
3. Bhuwan Singh: 41 years

End of Mahispal Dynasty

According to Bhasa Bansawali, there was a war between Mahispal and Kirant. From the east, Kirants attacked the Mahisapals and took the throne. Kirants was the third dynasty to rule Nepal, succeeding Mahispal and had the longest reign in Nepalese history, lasting over 1000 years.

CHAPTER II

Kirat Dynasty

Kirat Dynasty

Introduction

Kirat Dynasty is the third Dynasty to rule Nepal. Arguably, there are the longest reigning dynasty of Nepal. The Evidences and Knowledge of Kirat Dynasty as Kings of Nepal is much larger than Gopal and Mahispal Dynasty.

Kirat Dynasty is important because they had structured administrative practices and Legal System as well.

Origin of Kirat's

1. Rajaram Subedi mentioned that Kirats were Aryans who migrated to the eastern hills and steep regions of Nepal. They are called different because they live in hilly areas far from civilizations.
2. Another group of historians claims that Kirat arrived in Nepal around 2400 B.C.E., or 4400 years ago, after traveling east from Mesopotamia.
3. Another claim about the Kirat is that they arrived in Nepal from Tibet and China, which justifies their mongoloid facial structure. Kirats migrated to the eastern hills of Nepal from Tibet and started living there.

Kingship

The Kirat Dynasty took over the Mahispal Dynasty through brutal warfare. As Kirat lived in the eastern regions of Nepal, they managed to attack the Mahispal Dynasty from the east and brutally end the Mahispal Dynasty's reign. Yalamber was the valiant king who spearheaded the efforts to conquer Nepal.

Chronology

Visiting the chronicles, three general data points on how long the Kirat Dynasty reigned can be observed. Kirkpatrick wrote that 27 Kirat kings ruled Nepal for 1630 years. In Gopalraja Bansawali or the family tree, 32 Kirat Kings ruled for over 2180 years, whereas Daniel Wright mentions 29 Kirat Kings that ruled Nepal for 1132 Years. They can be considered to have ruled Nepal from 700 B.C.E to 300 C.E.

Important Kings

1. King Yalambar

King Yalambar, without any controversy, is the founder of the Kirat Dynasty in Nepal and the first Kirat King of Nepal. Patan was given the name Yala because of his surname.

His most important legacy is that Akash Vairav and its mask are worshiped during Indrajatra, a festival in the Kathmandu Valley. The mask is said to be that of King

Yalamber.

2. King Jitedasti

King Jitedasti, or Dasti, was the son of Humati, according to Wright's chronicle, and the seventh Kirat king of Nepal. King Jitedasti is famous because Buddha was rumored to have come to Nepal during his time.

3. King Stuko

King Stuko was the 16th king of Nepal. It has been mentioned that Emperor Ashoka and his daughter Charumati had arrived in Nepal. Then, Emperor Ashoka married his daughter to a Kshetriya named Devpal. Also, Chabahil, an area in Kathmandu, is rumored to have been named after Charumati herself.

Administration of Kirat Dynasty

Introduction

Only Few Structural Evidences are found about The Administration of Kirat Dynasty. It is the lost reigning dynasty in the History of Nepal. According to The Chronicle of Daniel Wright, 29 Kirat Kings ruled Nepal for over 1132 years. King Yalamber is the founding King and also the most popular King of Kirat Dynasty.

The Administration of Kirat Dynasty can be roughly divided into two Parts.

1. Administrative Tribunals
2. Administrative Position

Administrative Tribunals

1. Kuther

Kuther was an administrative office that collected State Revenue through Land and organized works related to Land and Taxation. Kuther was active during Lichhavi Dynasty as well.

2. Sholla

Sholla was a Judicial Administrative Office that dealt with Pancha Aparadh or Five Heinous Crimes and other Important Legal Matters

3. Ligwal

Ligwal dealt with the activities of Development and Trade in Kirat Period.

4. Mapchowk

Mapchowk was a Judicial Administrative Office that dealt with matter of Marriage, Divorce. It had very strict laws.

Administrative Positions

1. King

King or Hang was the Divine Head of the State or Government. He was provided with many powers that was regulated by the Ministers.

2. Ministers

Swami Prapannacharya has mentioned Eight Ministers that could have existed in Kirat Dynasty. He has called it "Astha Prakriti". They are:

1. Dhristi or Prime Minister 2. Jayanta or Foreign Minister 3. Bijaya or Defence

Minister 4. Surastra or Home Minister 5. Rastrabardhan or Development Minister 6.

Akhop or Law Minister 7. Dharmapal or Religious Minister 8. Sumantra or Finance Minister

3. National Assembly or Chumlung

- This Assembly has the highest Assembly of The Kirat's. It consisted of King, Ministers, Army and other Elected Officers of the State.
- Chumlung took important National Decisions.

The Chumlung consisted of Seater, Writer, Leader or Speaker of the Assembly and so on.

Conclusion

The Basic Structure of Nepal's Administration consisted of Offices and Officers. There were four Major Tribunals as well as other part of administrative positions in the Kirat Dynasty. The King didn't have absolute Power and was regulated by these Positions. Interestingly, The Tribunals were also Independent in nature and weren't affiliated to the State only.

Legal System of Kirat Dynasty

Introduction

Kirat Dynasty is Nepal is considered as the longest reigning Dynasty in Nepalese History. Daniel Wright's Chronicle states that Kirats ruled for 1132 years with 29 kings. Despite reigning for such lengthy periods, there are few evidences known about Kirat reign in Nepal.

The Legal System of Kirat Dynasty also suffers from the same Fate. Not much is known about it. But, what is known is that without law and Justice Society transforms to anarchy. Thus, there were some guides, some rules that paved the way for solving disputes and providing remedies. Similar was the case of Kirant Dynasty. They had a certain way of acting, behaving and so on.

The proof that Kirants had a Justice System lies in the very fact that Ancient Courts such as Kuther, Sulli, Ligwal and Mapchowk are derived from Kiranti language as well.

ShambhuPrasad Gyawali states that every Dynasty in Nepal is famous for at least one King who provided Justice to Nepali People. In the Kirant Dynasty, it was King Yalamber Hang. He is accepted as the first King of Nepal. According to Gopalraja Bansawali, he ruled for a historical 90 years.

Mundhum

Moving On, Kirant Legal System was based on Kirant Mundhum or Kirant Mundhum Khatun. It is said to be Vedas of the Kirant. Mundhum was transferred through words and passed for Generations similar to Vedas. After remembering the Vedas, People were supposed to act and behave according to it. These actions and behaviors are based on Customary Law that has been built according to Mundhum.

On Incest

A story in Mundhum: This is the story of Surunge Lalange and Laha Chhegna. Surunge Lalange was the brother of Laha Chhegna, sister. They were the children of First-born Individuals of Earth. As moving generation is deemed important, they copulated as there was no one else. When God found out about them, he gave the curse that they would turn into Ashes. But, Lalange convinced God that everyone are children from the same ancestor, hence, Incest would be everywhere. So, the rules were set for Seven Generations. After Seven Generations no one could commit incest. Those who did incest would be hunted down and Killed by God. Hadnata or Paternal relation and Dudhnata or Maternal Relations are to be pure. This was how the rules for Incest were set out.

On Birth and Death

If a son is born then his rites such as Nwaran must be completed in the Fourth Day. If a daughter is born then her rites must be completed in the Third Day. After these are completed, the women and the children become pure. Regarding Menstruation, if a Women bathes, washes her clothes, only then is she pure.

If a man dies, then he must be mourned for four days. If a woman dies, then she must be mourned for three days. If a child dies then the child's final rites must be completed the same day. The Home where the person died must omit themselves from any celebrations and festivals for a whole year.

On Justice

Justice is considered as the first virtue or object of Law. If Justice stops prevailing, then Humans will start killing each other like Birds and Humanity shall end. For Justice, Dharma is necessary, else the one who wrecks law shall be hated by God. They shall die early. So, to ensure Justice, a thoughtful Mukhiya or leader must be selected for every village by the villagers. That person shall treat everyone

Justly.

On Disputes

If intra-family conflict occurs, then the brothers should go to Tumyang or Subba. They shall initiate a Meeting and discussion. This form of Problem-solving shall be the best way of settling disputes and getting True Justice.

In the State, the King has the right to provide Justice. He has to listen to the case in front of all the ministers. The ministers should do and act to the best interest of the

Society. According to the ministers or Sabha's decision, The King shall also express his decision. If the decision made by Minister's is False, then God shall punish them.

On Conducts or Actions

Thieving, Looting, Fighting, Deceiving, Fooling, Pride, Greed, Provocative Behavior, Ensuing Chaos etc. shouldn't be done. Manipulation, Lying, Killing, Treating Orphans, Widows and Poor unjustly, Incest is always hated by God. Those people who busy themselves with these actions are not loved by God. They loosen the Fabric of Society and builds mistrust. Speaking Evil and Acting Evilly should be prohibited. Hence, these actions shall be punished. Similar to Bentham's doctrine of Fear, Legal Historians presume Fear was the sanction behind and no clear Punishment existed.

On Punishment

Killing should be punished with Death. Theft should be punished by putting the hands of thief in boiling Water. Then the Thief should be taken to Temple or any place of God. He/she should take an oath against Theft. Large Scale Theft and Looting should be punished with Organ Mutilation. If the thief or Looter cannot pay what has been looted then additional Charges should be provided. Those that betray the Nation or Rajadroha was punishable by

Exile.

Hadfora or Paternal Incest should be punished with Lifetime Slavery. Dudhfora or Maternal Incest should be punished with Exile from Home into a Cave.

If Evidence is not present then the Suspected should take an oath while touching and eating Mud of Earth.

Five Heinous Crimes such as Theft or Looting, Incest, Rajdroha or Treason, Homicide and Abetment or Encouragement of These Crimes were looked and decided after by The King himself. Other Crimes were decided upon by Local Authorities.

On Marriage

Marriage can be conducted by two different ways:

1. Traditional Limbu Method
2. By Taking Away the Girl for Marriage and conducting Marriage through Limbu Traditions

Divorce was allowed for well-being of Marriage and marital relations. For divorce purposes Sinko-Pangro or Stick had to be broken.

If Married Woman is taken away then, the suffering man or Sadhu could kill the Jar, the one who takes away the Female. The King would also provide all of the property of the Jar to Sadhu for re-marriage.

CHAPTER III

Lichhavi Dynasty

Lichhavi Dynasty

Introduction

Lichhavi Dynasty is known for Introducing Golden Ages in Nepal. Rishikesh Shah believes that there is a consensus among historians that the Lichhavi era commenced in Nepal by the 1st or 2nd century C.E., i.e., 50–200 B.S. Jayadeva the First was the first Lichhavi King of Nepal. He is known in history as a victor and a charismatic king.

Important Kings

1. King Vrsadeva: He built the Temple of Syambunath.

2. King Manadeva (464-505 C.E.): Manadeva started the Period of Written History in Nepal. Manadeva also ended revolutions from Local States and allegedly built Changunarayan Temple. He also prevented his mother, Rajyavati from going Sati.

Manadev built beautiful art and architecture during his reigns, such as Managriha and Manabihar. He started circulating coins named Manankas and had a picture of his wife, Bhogini.

3. King Amshuverma (605-621 C.E.): Amshuverma promoted the concept of Decentralized Governance or Self-Governance to Local Grams. He started the New Nepal

Sambat as well. He built an alternative to Managriha (Lichhavi's) called Kailashkuta Bhawan.

He circulated coins named SRI Amsu as well. He is also known to have been a diplomatic man who maintained relations between Tibet and India.

4. King Narendradeva (643-649 C.E.): Narendradeva freed Nepal from Courtiers who manipulated the King bringing Independence to the Rulers. He also helped The Emperor of China by sending 7000 men as assistance.

Due to the continuous relations between Nepal, China, and India, Nepal had become the center of trade and education. Learning of Sanskrit was widespread, and astrology and astronomy boomed in Nepali scholarly texts at the time of Narendradeva. He also created a Palace of his own.

5. King Jayadeva II (713–733 C.E.): King Jayadeva II wrote the famous Chronology of Lichhavi Kings in Pashupatinath Temple.

6. King Gunakamadeva (980-998 C.E.): King Gunakamadeva ruled during the Dark Ages of Nepal. Gunakamadeva is said to have founded the city of Kantipur, now Kathmandu. Gunakamadeva was the King who built Kasthamandap. He is supposed to have made huge donations to Pashupatinath. He also built the famous Sundhara. He circulated Gunanaka Coins as well.

Administration of Lichhavi Dynasty

Introduction

The Administration of Lichhavi Dynasty has the characteristics of Decentralization. The Country is divided into many tiers and such tiers function according to the Command of the Central Government. There were important Tribunals and Positions during the Lichhavi Dynasty as well.

Administrative Tribunals

1. Kuther: Collection of State Revenue
2. Sulli or Sholla: Five Heinous Crimes, *Lekhyadan*, Other Legal Matters
3. Ligwal: Development Activities
4. Mapchowk: Marriage, Divorce etc.
5. Paschimadhikaran : Situated in the Western Gate; Associated with Western Region; Protection of Temples, Religious Activities and Management of Disputes
6. Purvadhikaran: Situated in the Eastern Gate; Associated with Eastern Region
7. Bhattadhikaran : Prevention of Religious Anarchy (Dharmasankar); Make People follow their Occupation according to Varna Vyavastha; Governed and Decided by Wise Brahmins

Administrative Positions

1. King: The Lichhavi Kings exercised significant Power over the nation. Any decision required the certification of the King.
2. Antarasan or Paramasan: An Assembly formed under the leadership of the King; maintain balance and mediate disputes of Villages (Grams); the most superior assembly of the state.
3. Mahapratihar: Bodyguard and Right Hand of the King, similar to Hajuriya in Rana Regime; Very Powerful and Trusted by the King; Provided All Information to the King.

4. Pratihar: Found in Every Villages (Gram); provided latest news to Mahapratihar
5. Sarvadandanayak: The Administrative Chief of the Nation; Power to Punishment and other Legal Decisions. (Mahapratihar and Sarvadandanayak were given to the same man by The King)
6. Dandanayak: Handled Disputes and Battles; Punitive Power in small disputes; Worked under Sarvadandanayak
7. Mahabaladakshya : Army General or Commander-in-Chief of Army; Same respect as the Crown Prince
8. Dutak: Communicator of Kings Orders and Decisions to the General Public; Highly Trusted by the King (Crown Prince in most of the cases)
9. Kumaramatya : Chief Adviser to the Prince
10. Mahasamanta: Someone that controlled many Grams and Territories with exclusive rights
11. Samanta: Someone that had exclusive right over a certain territory.

Decentralization of Power

A. Lowest- Gram: It is a Large yet Separately located village or habited area. Gram is run by collection of five people's Council known as Panchali. The members of Panchali were known as Panchalik's. They had two major Duties:

1. Bring Water Tunnel, Make Places for Travellers to Rest etc.
2. Solve Local Disputes if they have the right to Self-Governance

B. Tala: The Combination of Various Gram's in Plain Area. The Administrative Rights of Tala was given
C. Drang: The Combinations of Gram and Tala
D. Highest- Center: It is ruled by the King.

Legal System of Lichhavi Dynasty

Lichhavi Dynasty is renowned in Nepal for building unfathomable Arts and Architecture. Reigning over Nepal for a glorious period of nearly 1000 years,

Lichhavi's introduced the Golden Era of Nepal. With Lichhavi's begun History of Nepal and with Lichhavi's ended the History of Ancient Nepal. Through various Inscriptions and other Evidences, The Legal History of Lichhavi Dynasty can be reckoned.

Lichhavi Kings although accepted and tolerated other Religions as well, they were primarily Hindus either the cult of Shaivism or Vaishnavism. Thus, their legal codes were also based on Hinduism and Hindu domain of Knowledege

Law and Punishment During Lichhavi Dynasty

Official Language of Lichhavi Kings was Sanskrit Language. Official Codes of Justice were Shastras and Dharmashastras. If Dharmashastras were not enough then Rajagya Sanad were issued by the King. According to Shambhu Prasad Gyawali, King Manadev-I was famous for his dispension of Justice. With exception of King Manadev, King Amshuverma and King Narendradeva were also famous Lichhavi Kings who contributed to Legal and Judicial Development of Nepal.

In an Inscription found in Hadigaon, Manusmriti, Yamasmriti, Brihaspatismriti, and Shukrasmriti were highly in use at the time. Also, when Kings were unable due to any circumstances in Justice Dispension, then Highly educated Brahmin and their assembly were called for this purpose. The Brahmins were expected to be lawful and blind in the investigation of cases and provide impartial decisions.

Several Basis for Punishment existed. The Amount of Punishment, Mens Rea of Punishment, Time, Place, Power of Alleged Criminal, Nature of Crime and Economic Conditions were the factors in deciding cases.

Forms of Punishment

So, what were the Punishment? Unlike Modern times when Compensation and Imprisonment are the Prime Punishment. Lichhavi Period had four forms of Punishment.

First was Bhakdanda. Bhakdanda means Punishment through Scolding. This was given when the alleged committed small magnitude of Punishment. This was done as to provide the criminal the right Guidance so as to prevent further Punishment.

Second was Dhikdanda. Dhik Danda was similar to De-Motivation or Destroying one's reputation through Public Shaming. Dhikdanda was basically making the criminal feel guilty and thus hoping that they wouldn't repeat any sort of Crime for the Second time.

Third was Arthadanda. Arthadanda was similar to today's Financial Compensation. Financial Compensation was used to instigate fear for one's future of Living a Good Life and was not aimed at any forms of Reformation.

Fourth was Badhdanda. Badhdanda was extreme form of Punishment. Badhdanda meant Organ Mutilation as well as Death Penalty.

In the Inscription of Yangalhiti and Brihngareshwor, Theft, Looting, Killing, Treason, Misbehavior with Married

Females were strictly punished. Even the

Families of Criminals were punished. Later, Lichhavi King also loosened the Punishment later on. The Principle of Criminal Law that only the criminal shall be punished was not practiced. This practice was ended by Ram Shah and "Jasko Paap Usko Gardan" Principle. Even the Measurement System was checked every Six months.

Mapchowk Tribunal

Mapchowk was among the most important organs of Judicial Administration during Lichhavi Period. In an Inscription present in Mali Gaon, Marriage and Divorce were handled in Mapchowk itself. Mapchowk had a strict set of Punishment according to that inscription.

Rules on Marriage

If a Woman was not sexually satisfied or in any way satisfied with her Husband then she had the right to divorce and remarry.

A woman could divorce a man and remarry in these Conditions:

1. Death of Husband
2. Disappearance of Husband
3. If Husband becomes Saint or Sage
4. No Children
5. "Patit Bhayema"

But these was a condition for these divorces. The Woman who Remarried had to remarry. If the woman didn't give birth to a child, then the woman was punished or fined. If the woman took on multiple Husband and then didn't give birth then she was fined.

In the other hand, a man could make multiple wives and they wouldn't be punished. The only exception was Jari.

Jari meant running away with a married woman whose

Husband is alive and well. It was among Panchakhad or Five Great Crimes in Ancient Nepal. Even keeping a secret relation with a woman was punishable by Law.

Simply, A man could do anything but Jari and "Mistressing".

Marriage and Sexual Relations among Different Castes

As you know, Lichhavi Dynasty had a strict social hierarchy established by the Dharmashastras known as Varna Vyavastha. Society was divided into four classes. They are Brahmin, Kshetriya, Vaishya and Shudra respectively. One of the rules of Varna Vyavastha was that one class of society were supposed to marry their counterpart from same class. i.e. A Vaishya male could marry a Vaishya female only.

Thus, if imbalances were created in Varna Vyavastha then it was strictly punishable.

Sexual Misconduct on Same class of Female had Uttam Sahas or Simple Punishment.

Sexual Misconduct or Marriage of Higher-Class Male and Lower-Class Female was known as Anulom and it had medium Punishment or Madhyam Sahas.

Sexual Misconduct or Marriage of Lower-Class Male and Higher-Class Female was known as Pratilom and was punished the highest. Male could be given Death Penalty. Females had their Organ Mutilated as Females weren't given Death Penalty back in those days.

Paramasan or Antarasan

Paramasan was where the King was sitted. Paramasan was also a Quasi-Judicial Court. Paramasana decided cases that couldn't be decided by local Bodies or other Administration. They also looked after cases of Bhatta Tribunal and other Tribunals. Generally, when the

Tribunals were closed Paramasana looked after the cases.

Similar to the Supreme Court, it was the final Dispensator of Justice. It also reviewed Cases. It was similar to Judicial Assembly or Nyaya Sabha. Dwarik or Pratihar informed Judicial Assembly about the cases that had occurred throughout the Country.

This Judicial Assembly was also known as Dharmadhikaran or Dharma Tribunal. Why? Because it relied on Dharmashastras to dispense justice and dicuss about Economic Conditions of the Country. It can be called National Assembly as well. Chinese Travellor Huang Huen Tshe has mentioned about the Judicial Assembly during the Period of King Narendradeva.

Duties of National Assembly

1. Both the parties had to be heard Impartially.
2. According to Shukraniti, The decision had to be made according to the present state of Society, Societal Traditions and expert suggestions of Wise Men.
3. Only an Impartial, a knower of Dharmashastras and Vedas and Truthful Men could be made part of National Assembly.
4. Resolve the disputes and review cases that haven't been resolved by Local Panchayat. Mentioned in the Inscription of Narayansthan
5. National Assembly had to handle disputes among Local Panchayats in the case of Border disputes and so on.

Local or Gram Panchayats

The central Government couldn't handle every aspect and minor problems of

Administration. Hence, Local Panchayats were delegated significant Power and Rights in deciding Local disputes. Large Scale Cases and Pancha Aparadh were the only crimes that couldn't be looked out by Local Panchayats. This came with a cost though! Local Panchayats had to provide salary to their officers through their own Dandakunda. Some Villages were allowed to look after the cases of Pancha Aparadh. Shivadeva Inscription in Mangal Bazaar says that Mangal Bazaar will not be obstructed by Ligwal and Sulli in deciding cases of Pancha Aparadh. Local Panchayat were run by Panchas

The Panchas of Local levels were selected by the Kings. They had to decide cases, Punish Criminals, Provide Water and Water Tunnels to villagers, Construct and Care Religious Temples.

Similar to Village Municipality, Municipality, Sub-Metropolitan Municipality and so on, Gram, Tala and Drang existed in Kathmandu Valley and Saat Gaon's near it. In other places, only Local Gram Panchayat existed

Cases Handled Under Kathmandu Valley

Step 1: Gram Panchali or Local Panchayats

Step 2: Tala: Talaswami

Step 3: Drang

Step 4: Register to Dwarik or Mahapratihar

Step 5: Antarasana

Cases Handled under Eastern and Western Region

Step 1: Gram Panchali or Local Panchayats

Step 2: East Tribunal or West Tribunal

Step 3: Register to Dwarik or Mahapratihar (Inscription of Narayanchaur) Step 4: Antarasana

An Inscription in Khopashi mentions that one couldn't directly go to the King to solve disputes. So, a strict set of Hierarchy for Judicial Administration was set.

Criminal Justice System

Once the Alleged charges were finalized and the convicted was proven guilty, then they couldn't run away. If they ran away then the convicted were handled harsher Punishment

Another Important part of Lichhavi Criminal Justice System is Witness Testimony.

A witness couldn't be pressured or manipulated to speak for someone or provide untruthful Testimony. The one who does so or attempt to do so were also punished.

According to Narayanchowk Inscription, Unjust Ruling of Decision and Forceful Acceptance of Decision were also punished. Both Parties had to be satisfied by the decision to be finalized.

Conclusion and Analysis

Thus, there was an extensive Judicial Administration and its hierarchy in Lichhavi Period. It is characterized by Educated Judges and Lawful Dharmashastras.

Decentralization of Justice can also be observed. Division of Cases as well as Investigative Justice System can be observed during Lichhavi Dynasty. Punishment itself was divided. There were several factors on deciding Punishment and so on. Hence, The Legal System of Lichhavi Dynasty was much advanced and decentralized for its time which was in average 1500 years ago.

CHAPTER IV

Malla Dynasty

Malla Dynasty

Introduction

According to H.C. Roy It was Mallas from Ancient India that migrated to plains of Terai. They started to move along Bagmati river and started to settle there. Through the passing of time, Mallas settled in Kathmandu Valley itself and got their hands of Nepalese Kingship once the time was right.

Baburam Acharya argues that the Mallas that we know today as Kings of Kathmandu were another random Kshetriya race. They used the titular name of Malla. So, Ari Malla was the first King of Malla Dynasty. Another fact that Historians agree with is that Ari Malla became the King of Nepal in 1200 C.E.

Important Kings

Early Medieval Period

1. King Jayastithi Malla (1382-1395 C.E.): He drew up codes of religious and social conduct with the help of Five Brahmans. These codes are known as Nyaya Bikashini or ManabNyaya Shastra. It is supposed to have been written in 1380 C.E.

Jayastithi Malla introduced reforms in Land measurement, irrigation and agriculture. He brought strict rules and regulations against Theft, Incest etc. Jayastithi Malla also made sure that 4 classes or varna had their own rules and regulations including House-construction and so-on.

2. King Yaksha Malla (1428-1482 C.E.): He started the tradition of putting Bhatta's in charge of Pashupatinath. He built the Peacock Window, Dattareya. He extended the Borders of Nepal. After his reign, His sons divided Nepal into Four Kingdoms among which one was later merged.

Kingdom of Kantipur

1. King Mahendra Malla (1560-1574 C.E.): Mahendra Malla is known for two primary reasons. First, he also wrote various codes of social and religious conduct. Second, he is known for circulating silver coins known as Mahendramallikas. He did an agreement with Mugal Emperor to circulate Nepalese coins for Trade purposes. He brought silver and gold from Tibet and minted coins in Nepal, establishing successful trade relations. Also, he built Taleju Temple within his palace. He ruled from 1560 C.E. TO 1574 C.E.

2. King Pratap Malla (1641-1674 C.E.): He constructed Rani-Pokhari for his wife to console the death of their favourite Son Cakravartendra. In another context, He also donated valuables worth his weight in Pashupatinath in a highly talked about ceremony called Tuladana. He also brought into fame White Matsyendranath Dance which was practiced since 1627 C.E. He was known as the King of Poets.

3. King Jayaprakash Malla (1734-1768 C.E.): He was the Last Malla King of Kantipur.

Kingdom of Patan

1. King Siddhinarsimha Malla (1618-1661 C.E.): Siddinarsimha is remembered for constructing Krishna Mandir in front of the Royal Palace in 1636 A.D. Overall, he was a friendly and a religious King who introduced peace and prosperity in Patan. He is also known for his Diplomacy with Gorkha and Indian Plains.

Kingdom of Bhadgaon

1. King Bhupatindra Malla (1696-1722 C.E.): He is well known for major contributions in arts, poetry and architecture. It was Bhupatindra Malla who built the temple of Nyatapola in Bhaktapur. He also built a water passing Channel in Thimi. He also had a glass pane window in his palace that was very rare and amazing. He constructed a mini temple of Taleju Bhavani. He erected a bronze statue of himself, erected an image of Akash Bhairav in the palace square.

2. King Ranajita Malla (1722-1769 C.E.): Ranajita Malla had the border till

Dudhkoshi River in the east and his territory reached Dolakha. He printed coins in his name to hint the beginning of his reign. Ranjita Malla also had a long reign that lasted from 1722 C.E. to 1769 C.E.

Administration of Malla Dynasty

Introduction

After the Ascension of Malla Dynasty in Nepal, The Local Bodies were given High Independence and the Center controlled only few of the administrative works. Tribunals such as Mapchowk, Ligwal had become irrelevant. Thus, there were some differences in the Sddministration of Malla Dynasty than its predecessors. The Administration also had a hierarchy due to

Decentralization of Power.
Central Administration Positions

1. King: The King had absolute right and Power over the complete set of affairs of a nation including Law making, application of policies and Judicial tasks.
2. Sachib: The Prime Advisor and Assistant to the King
3. Dharmadhikari: The Most Trusted and Educated Brahmin that served the King; Settled Important Cases relating to Dharma
4. Crown Prince: Worked as Prime Minister or Administrator to the King (Sometimes)
5. Amatya or Praman: Member of Sachib Mandal
6. Mahapatras: Seven Ancestral Aristocratic Families of the Region that fought for Power with the King

Organizations

1. Bhardari Assembly: Consisted of Important Administrators and other Government Officers such as Kaji, Chautara, and other Ministers.
2. Ordinary Assembly: Consisted of Normal People; called for making important national decisions.
3. Sachib Mandal: Resembles Council of Ministers; Prime Minister or Mulkaji leaded the Cabinet. Prime Minister was also called Mahamatya, Mahamantridhiraj etc.
4. Senadhakshya: Army General or Commander-in-Chief of Army

Province Administration

1. Mahasamanta or Samanta: The Major Administrators of Provinces; Hereditary right over a Province; if many

provinces are captured then they become Mahasamanta.

2. Dware and Charridware: They transmitted information to the King. They were called Pratihar in Lichhavi Era. They also collected evidences and adjudicated cases.
3. Bishyapati: Powerful ruler of Provinces
4. Praman: Governed and Directed Provinces as well as Local Bodies; Authority in making decisions against cases

Others: Mahamandalik, Pramukh, Praman, Pradhan, etc. as well

Local Administration

The Local Areas were divided into Tol, Desh and Gram.

Gram: Gram were ruled over by Panchasamuchhaya. They are similar to Panchali's of Lichhavi Dynasty.

Desh: Developed Towns were called Desh in those days. It was governed by Desh Nayak. Desh in the border of another state was ruled by Kotnayak.

Tol: Tol was governed by Tolnayak or Twarnayak.

Judicial Administration

The Central Authority of Judicial System was King. The Kings were followed by Amatya's or Ministers. They also made some decisions.

There were two major Courts to handle cases near the Kathmandu Valley.

- Kotling: Located in the Center of Kathmandu; Dealth with Civil Cases; administered by Nyayakari; Future Appeal to King; Acted as an Appeal Court
- Itchapali: Dealt with Criminal Cases and Pancha Aparadh;

Below these Courts were Local Bodies who had the right to Self-Governance. They settled cases Locally.

Legal System of Malla Dynasty

After the end of Lichhavi Era, the Legal System of Nepal was more chaotic than ever. With Amshuverma, decentralization policy had been implemented to the fullest and the tribunals were given minimum rights over local bodies. Hence, Nepal was effectively divided. The once large Nepal started to lose its territory and was nearly limited to the Kathmandu Valley itself. The time for strictness both from external invasion and internal irregularity seemed to be the necessity of the time. This feat was achieved by the most famous King of Malla Dynasty.

'Jayastithi Raja Malla'

In short, Jayastithi Malla introduced reforms in Land measurement, irrigation and agriculture. He brought strict rules and regulations against Theft, Incest etc. Jayastithi Malla also made sure that 4 classes or varna had their own rules and regulations including House-construction and so-on.

Gopalraja Bansawali

Gopalraja Bansawali mentions that Pashupatinath Temple was looted during the reign of Jayastithi Malla. This looting was more vicious than the attacks of Jitari Malla and his successors. Hence, Jayastithi Malla or Stithi Malla promulgated laws to give death Penalty to thieves and introduced strict set of rules and regulations against theft and other crimes. He made Dharmashastras and Smriti's as his basis for these laws. This resulted in abolition of Theft in Kathmandu Valley according to the Gopalraja Bansawali.

Bhasa Bansawali

Stithi Malla promulgated four major types of Laws in Nepal.

1. **Housing Laws or Griha Nirnaya**
2. **Area Laws or Kshetra Nirnaya**
3. ***Jaat* Laws or Jaat Nirnaya**
4. **Manab Nyaya Shastra: The Code of Human Justice**

Housing Laws

Griya Nirnaya mentions the importance of houses in Cities, Road and Streets.

1. Caste will decide the types of houses built and the neighborhood where they are built.
2. Brahmins and Newar's of Higher Caste should build their houses near the King's Palace. Anyone other than the Higher Castes will be punished.
3. Big Businessmen could also make houses near the King's Palace. They had to be built out of bricks and Special Waterproof Rooftops or *Ghingti.*
4. Lower Caste should live in a grouped area similar to Ghettos and should make their houses without Good Rooftops.

Area Laws

Kshetra Nirnaya mentions necessity and division of lands according to their productivity.

1. Land is divided into Abbal, Doyam, Sim and Chahar according to its productivity.

2. Ksetrakar should conduct the measurement of lands and divide likewise.
3. Takshakar should conduct the measurement of Houses.
4. Irrigation Tunnel, Irrigation Facilities, Its Division and Maintainance were also mentioned.

Jaat Laws

Jaat Laws reinforced the necessity of Occupational Structure which had disappeared in Nepal. Varna Vyavastha as it is known, designates a person with their ancestral occupation. The absence of such structure is known as Dharmasankar.

1. Kshetriya serving in Military, Chitrakar in artistic works, Salmi in Oil Extraction, Nau in cutting hair, Sukhal in carrying People and so on were written about 64 types of Jaat's. All had to do what they were designated to do.
2. From Birth to Death, one had to conduct their life according to their Jaat.

The Code of Human Justice

Stithi Malla brought five Brahmins from Mithila and South India and formed a legal body under the leadership of Minister Jait Burma. They had studied Manusmriti, Yagyabalkyasmriti, Mitakshara Tika, Naradsmriti, Brihaspati Smriti, Shukra Niti etc. They adopted the rightful laws acceptable and enforceable in the then society and constructed a set of laws known as Manab Nyayashastra or Code of Human Justice. This was also known as Narad Samhita. Narad Samhita was written by Maharishi Narad. It has 14 Chapters and discusses a wide array of legal matters from Judicial Procedures to Division of Property.

According to Bhasa Bansawali, Varna Vyavastha was exclusively applied in Nepal from 1445 B.S. to 1452 B.S. National Archive has an inscription that says that it was written in 1437 B.S. by the King of Bhaktapur, Stithi Malla.

Despite writing the laws and codes of conducts, Stithi Malla did not exclusively mentioned neither the Legal System nor the Judicial Administration practiced at the time. Historians believe that Malla's inherited the Judicial Administration of the Lichhavi Kings with the presence of few and slight modifications.

Pratap Malla on Justice

Pratap Malla introduced some legal reforms in Nepal. Oath by touching Kal Bhairav was prevalent. Many died due to the 'Religious' power of Kal Vairav and hence, it was stopped. He believed that a case arises only when one doesn't adhere to dharma. Hence, the judge should take an oath before Kotlingeshwor that he will be just in his judgement. The Stone of Justice was touched during the Oath. For Pratap Malla's Contribution, he was remembered as 'Dharmaraj Nepaleshwor'.

An Overview of Judicial Administration during Mallas Major Judicial Administrators

Chautara or P.M. became powerful during Malla Dynasty through the imitation of Muslim States. Chautara, Pramans and Kaji's were provided their 'Pagari', a symbolic Head-ware of their Administrative Rank.

Centre > Praman or Maha Patras> Desh Nayak > Dware > Kotwar > Tahasildar

Mahane Adda caught criminals and protected forests or Van Durga's.

Janapadas

The Local Body or Gram was run by Panchayat or Pancha Valadmi. They were known as Panchalik's in

Lichhavi Period. They sorted out the quarrels and prevalent local cases. If any sort of dissatisfaction or opposition arose of such decision, then the citizens could, through Praman or Pratihars access the central court of the King. The Praman would evaluate the case and present it in front of the King. Chadidar or Daudaha were also present for easy and speedy communication of Justice. This developed a set of Judicial Hierarchy in Nepal. This method was applied to the citizens outside Kathmandu. They were known as Janapadas.

Paur

For citizens inside the Kathmandu Valley, there were two primary courts. One was Kotling and the other was Itachapali.

Kotling and Itchapali Adalat

According to Hudson, Itachapali and Kotling were the major forms of Central Courts in Nepal. They were based on ancient form of practices and regulations. Kotling was a civil court and Itchapali was a criminal court.

Property, Division of Property, Transaction and Business-related cases were handled by Kotling Court.

Itachapali was the highest court for criminal offence. Murder or Death, Theft and Looting, Cow-Killing, Treason etc. were dealt by this court. They were the court of Second Instance. The First Instance Adda was that of Praman and the final instance was that of King.

Manabnyayashastra

On Marriage

One could marry within their jaat and inter-jaat marriage was prohibited. This was done to continue the adherence to Varna Vyavastha. Inter-jaat Marriage was divided into two types:

1. Anulom Marriage: If a higher Jaat male married a lower Jaat female, then it was Anulom. If the Jaat could drink water from each other, then it wasn't punished severely. However, one had to purify themselves after eating Food from such Female.

2. Pralom Marriage: If a higher Jaat female married a lower jaat male, then it was Pralom. This sort of marriage had strict punitive consequences. The male who married such women was either given death penalty (In Extreme Situations) or had his organ mutilated.

Other Laws on Marriage

1. If a Brahmin started living together with a widowed-Brahmin women, then he was just imposed fine.

Sexual Relations

2. If a Higher Jaat female had sexual relations with Lower Jaat male, then the female would have 'Jaat Patit'. Her Jaat would become that of the male with whom she had sexual relations.

3. If a Higher Jaat male had sexual relation with untouchable or untouchable and unacceptable then, the male would have his Jaat patit, similar to that of the female. If the women was acceptable then Jaat patit wouldn't happen.

4. If a brahmin had sexual relations with Untouchable and acceptable, then he was fined Rs. 120 with Rs. 24 as Contemplation Punishment. After the Contemplation Punishment, the Brahmin had to do fasting to become pure. If a Kshetriya or Shudra committed such crimes, he would be fined half the amount i.e. Rs.60.

Jari

5. If Jari was committed i.e. Male committing sexual misconducts on married women, he was fined Rs. 60. Some Jaat even had the practices of cutting and killing Jaar although most of the castes didn't. If Shudra committed such crimes, they would be punished 4 times or 5 times as much.

Others

6. If a Brahmin kept someone who wasn't Brahmin or Kshetrita then he would be punished or imprisoned.

Evidence Analysis

Generally, Primary Evidences including Witness and other Physical Evidences were admissible to the court in the first instance. However, Primary Evidences were scarce. When Primary Evidences were insufficient or lacking in some manner, Dibya Sapath or Ordeal was taken. Ordeal was relied upon on higher or weightier cases only.

Five Types of Ordeal System existed at the time.

1. Ordeal of Fire Entry
2. Ordeal of Poison Consumption
3. Ordeal of Weight Comparison
4. Ordeal of Water Drowning

Ordeal is observed with contempt and disdain for its sheer reliance on luck and faith. It was abolished by Muluki Ain, 2010. Rewati Raman Khanal, writes that Ordeals were Psycho-Religious in nature. He argues that such form of Punishment could be justified in the society of the time. Only strong had to face ordeals and disabled were excluded. However, he fails to recognize that negative aspects of such forms of punishments. P.N. Shah killing the Jaishi's of Belkot through Ordeal is glorified by Rewati Raman Khanal when it should be condemned for one's life is much important than sheer luck.

Evidence Dismissal

The cases during Malla period were swift and not delayed. Witness Evidence would not be lost and False Evidence would not be created. Large Crimes were responsed with Death Penaltyor Scarce Imprisonment. Small evidences were dealt with through Economic Punishment.

Basis of Punishment

The punishment system was based on Jaat Vyavastha. The harshest punishment on

Brahmin would be 'Char Pata Mudera Desh Nikala Garnu'. Basically, Exile after Cutting hair in an embarrassing way i.e. To remind society of the person's crime. For Kshetriya to Shudra's, it was Organ Mutilation or even Death Punishment.

Imprisonment was not the preferred means of Punishment. During the early Lichhavi Period, Economic Punishment was used. But, after providing autonomy to Local Panchalik's to get the compensation, Central Government didn't find it feasible as the economic benefits would go to the Panchaliks not them. Hence Physical Punishment were preferred. Deterrence and Fear of Commision of Crime was the rationale behind it.

Procedure of Punishment

If a Just is punished and unjust is left unpunished, Gods were believed to have sent the Judges and Kings to Hell itself. The Judges would be shamed in front of the public as well. So, they generally collected stacks of evidences before declaring the criminal and the punishment. Hence, some criminals could escape without harm.

Types of Punishment

1. Bak Danda or Counselling
2. Dhik Danda or Defamation
3. Artha Danda or Economic Compensation
4. Karavas or Imprisonment
5. Anga Chedan or Organ Deformation
6. Anga Bhanga or Organ Mutilation
7. Badh Danda or Death Penalty

Five Heinous Crimes or Pancha Maha-Patak

According an inscription in Nuwakot by Prithivendra Malla, The five heinous crimes are:

1. Kin Murder 2. Child Murder 3. Female Murder 4. Teacher Murder 5. Unfaithfulness Towards Ancestry

According to an inscription in Motihar by Abhaya Malla, The Five Heinous Crimes are: 1. Kin Murder 2. Child Murder 3. Female Murder 4. Brahmin's Murder 5. Kidnapping

These were not actually part of the punishment system but rather a sanction. The Sins that were obtained through these activites would be transferred if the said duty was not fulfilled by the person. An Inscription of Subhahal of Bishnusimha says that if the duties of Guthi are not fulfilled, then the persons responsible would suffer from Pancha Mahapatak.

Shah Dynasty

Shah Dynasty

Introduction

Dilli Raman Regmi writes that Shah Kings were descendants of Rajput Dynasty of Chittaud Kingdom. They arrived to Nepal after a dispute with The Muslim Emperor.

Their descendants became the King of Nuwakot. Kulmandan Shah, The King of

Nuwakot sent his son Yasobikram Shah to rule Lamjung. He had two sons: Narahari Shah and Drabya Shah. Drabya Shah was contacted by one of the courtiers of Gorkha to be the King of Gorkha. First, he defeated Ligligkot.

Drabya Shah Victory Over Ligligkot

Here is one of the most interesting stories on how Ghale's were defeated by Drabya Shah.

Ghale's of Ligligkot had a marathon race to decide who would be the King for one year. It happened every year on the day of Bijaya Dashami. So,

1. During The Race of Bijaya Dashami, Drabya Shah attacked the weaponless Ghale's and became the King of Ligligkot.

2. Drabya Shah was allowed to be part of the Race of Ghale because of his Weakness. He won the race and became The King of Nepal.

3. Drabya Shah provided Wine and Local Liqueurs to Ghale before the race. The Ghale's couldn't run properly and Drabya Shah won the race.

Victory over Gorkha

In 1559 C.E. he attacked Gorkha for the first time and failed. He attacked again by sneaking into Gorkha. Drabya Shah killed the Khadka King and finally became The King of Gorkha.

Unification Campaign of P.N. Shah

Prithvi Narayan Shah rose to the throne of Gorkha at the age of 20 in 1799 B.S. The Kingdom of Gorkha was expanded by Ram Shah and mini attempts were being made to conquer other Kingdoms. P.N. Shah being ambitious decided to conquer the Kingdoms surrounding Gorkha and ultimately Kathmandu Valley itself.

Pre-Unification

1. Before the Unification Campaign, Gorkha conducted a Treaty with Lamjung. P.N. Shah also had a failed marriage with the daughter of King of Makwanpur.

They devised a treaty whose major points are:

1. Gorkha and Lamjung should maintain a continuous brotherhood and friendship.
2. Gorkha shall assist Lamjung against its war on Kaski.

3. Lamjung shall not attack Gorkha if Gorkha starts attacking Eastern frontiers.

2. Diplomacy with Bhaktapur

Bhaktapur developed Diplomatic relations with one another. In 1741 C.E., the crown Prince of Gorkha travelled to Bhaktapur. P.N. Shah was made ritual Brother of the Crown Prince of Bhaktapur.

3.Battle of Nuwakot II: The Loss of Gorkha

In 1800 C.E., P.N. Shah sent an army under General Biraj Thapa Magar to attack Nuwakot. P.N. Shah had attacked Nuwakot with weak battalion, minimum weapons and without any significant strategy. Hence, he lost the battles with ease.

4. Military and Arms Re-Arrangement and Increment of Gorkha

P.N. Shah travelled to Kashi to gather Weapons. He implemented aggressive taxation policy and took Rs. 1 from each house to finance the expedition and weapons. After his return, he made it compulsory for the youth of 16 to 30 to participate in military activities in Gorkha.

5. The Treaty of Gorkha and Chaubise Kingdoms

The Final step P.N. Shah took before moving to the eastern front with his military was renew the Treaty with Lamjung. This was the Treaty of Dharma Bandej.

Unification Campaign

The Prime Events in his victory over Kathmandu Valley are as follows:

1. The Battle of Nuwakot III: The Victory of Gorkha

In 1744 C.E., Prithivi Narayan Shah and his military made up their minds to attack

Nuwakot. The best time for attack was set for 26th September. Hence, on 25th September night, the Army of

Gorkha crossed the Trishuli river and divided themselves into three parts.

In the morning, Kalu Pande and his army attacked Nuwakot. After the Gorkhali's became victorious, they gathered themselves and King P.N. Shah entered the Palace of Nuwakot.

At the end, after two unsuccessful attempts, Nuwakot was finally captured by Gorkha in 1744 C.E. This victory was beneficial economically due to trade, agriculturally due to fertile lands and politically due to better military position. Hence, P.N. Shah made his headquarters in Nuwakot forgetting his homeland completely.

2. The Battle of Nuwakot IV: The Victory of Gorkha

After Nuwakot was successfully captured, Shah planned on attacking Sakhu, Sindupalchowk, Kavrepalanchowk and Dolakha. He used the help of Ranajita Malla, The King of Bhaktapur and Thapa Clan.

For their contribution, Sakhu and Changu was returned to Ranajita Malla. Parshuram Thapa controlled Sindupalchowk, Kavrepalanchowk, Dolakha etc. P.N. Shah kept Namudam, Mahadevpokhari etc.

3. The Battle of Kirtipur I

P.N. Shah wanted to attack Kirtipur within 1858 C.E. So, he did. Nearly 1200

Soldiers under the leadership of Kalu Pande set determined to be a victor against Kirtipur. After 12 hrs Kalu Pande was hit by an arrow. Kalu Pande fainted and the rest of the Malla army Killed him. King Prithvi Narayan Shah gave the order to end the war accepting their defeat.

4. The Conquest of Makwanpur

Gorkhali soldiers marched to conquer Makwanpur in 1762 C.E. August 21. They defeated the Army and conquered Makwanpur. Later, they went to Hariharpurgadi and Timalkot to imprison the King Digbandhan Sen. The King escaped again. He went to Bengal Nawab and request an army which Gorkha defeated officially annexing Makwanpur. 5. Second Attack on Kirtipur

On 1764 December 16, Surpratap Shah Kaji Daljit Shah and Kaji Sriharsha Shah jointly representing Gorkha marched towards Kirtipur. However, Kirtipur, instead of battling closed its gates. As Kirtipur was surrounded with large walls and forts, it was impossible to penetrate Kirtipur. They failed and returned again.

5. Third Attack on Kirtipur

P.N. Shah decided to attack Kirtipur for the third time. The date of attack was 1765

B.S. May 10th. Kirtipur's walls were closed. They surrounded Kirtipur for Six whole months.

Finally, after 6 months the citizens of Kirtipur surrendered and Gorkhali's were provided the right to rule Kirtipur. The Official date is recounted to be 1766 C.E. 12th March.

6. Conquest of Kathmandu Valley

Kathmandu had a final weapon in its arsenal. East India Company. Jayaprakash pleaded East India Company to send their troops in defense of Kathmandu.

However, P.N. Shah's army defeated them in Sinduli Gadi and forced them to retreat.

After realizing that P.N Shah's victory was fixed and "destined", Jayaprakash fled to Patan in September 26th 1768.

In 1768 C.E., Jayaprakash Malla fled to Patan. Then, Tejnarasimha Malla with Jayaprakash Malla fled to Bhaktapur in the same year 1768 C.E.

P.N. Shah conqured Patan and Kathmandu in 1768 C.E. On 10th November 1769

C.E., Gorkhali Troops entered Bhaktapur from the eastern gate. Bhatapur had housed Three Kings and after battling for two days, they surrendered because Jayaprakash was injured by a musket ball. Finally, Bhaktapur was also annexed. Thus, Prithvi Narayan Shah became the First King of Modern Nepal.

Pre-Rana Regime History

Rajendra Laxmi

Prithvi Narayan Shah died in 1831 B.S. at the age of 52. His son Pratap Singh Shah became the King of Nepal. He also died in 1834 B.S. After the Death of Pratap Singh Shah, Rajendra Laxmi Shah became the sole regent queen of Nepal from 1836 B.S. until she died in 1842 B.S.

Some major events and territorial gains happened during her reign. She improved

Nepal's relations with the British East India Company and introduced peace and safety in Nepal. She repelled a rebellion in Vijayapur (a kingdom in the east conquered by P.N. Shah) in 1839 B.S.

The conquest of Nepal took on new forms, and the territory of Nepal was extended to the Kaligandaki river. The kingdoms of Lamjung, Kaski, Tanahu, Nuwakot, Dhor, Pauju, Rupakot, Charikot, etc. were integrated under Nepal.

Bahadur Shah

After the death of Rajendra Laxmi Shah in 1842 B.S., Bahadur Shah' (Brother of Pratap Singh Shah) acted as Regent for Rana Bahadur Shah. Bahadur Shah, within seven years of being Regent, extended the Western Borders of Nepal to Yamuna. He showed excellent traits of a Leader, Diplomat and Administrator in these Seven Years. He defeated Baise Kingdoms, Kumau, Gadhwal as well as

Kangada reaching the highest point of Nepalese Conquest. He was removed from the post of Regent and assassinated in 1854 B.S.

Rana Bahadur Shah

Rana Bahadur Shah was the son of Pratap Singh Shah and Rajendra Laxmi Shah. He was also the grandson of Prithvi Narayan Shah. He became King at the age of two years old when his father died. Rana Bahadur Shah made his son Givarna Yuddha Bikram Shah King of Nepal in 1855 B.S after the signature of 95 Bhardars or Courtiers. It was due to the pressure of his dying wife.

Rana Bahadur Shah fled to Kashi after being attacked by his courtiers. He returned in 1860 B.S. Falgun and got absolute Power. He was the First Mukhtiyar of Nepal. He was assassinated in 1863 B.S. by his brother and Bhimsen Thapa became the Mukhtiyar of Nepal.

Bhimsen Thapa

Bhimsen Thapa ruled as Mukhtiyar from 1863 B.S. to 1894 B.S. Bhimsen Thapa conducted the final advance on the Unification of Nepal. Under Amarsingh Thapa, the fort of Kangada was seized for three years A sikh army under Ranajita Sigh finally defeated Amarsingh Thapa. This meant that Nepal was limited to the Satalaja River. This was the last unification campaign of Nepal.

Bhimsen Thapa brought Social Reforms in Nepal. He restricted Slavery. He also brought systematic Taxation and Measurement System. He reforemed various inhuman marriage practices. He promoted the Policy of Free Trade. He also introduced Hierarchy in Administration with regulated Salary. He also introduced reforms in Military.

Bhimsen Thapa stabbed himself after being imprisoned in 1896 B.S. Shrawan 8. He died nine days later. Bhimsen Thapa was imprisoned by the then King Rajendra Bikram

Shah.

The Legal System of Ram Shah

Major Administrators

King > Chautara > Minister or Kaji > Commander-in-Chief or Senapati or Sardar > Khajanchi and Kapardar and Kharidar

26 Thithis

Ram Shah passed "The 26 *Thithi*" or *Dhog Bhet Thithis*. He also passed on other laws that are yet to be known or discovered. He passed 26 laws known as the 26 Thithis. The King would also pass laws on necessity through *Sanadpatra, Rajagya* and *Rukka*. After Unification, Local Laws were passed by the King as per request through Sanad, Sawal and Rajagya.

On Royal Meetings

1. The King or Shri 5 must be addressed 'सरकार प्रभ ' or Lord Majesty.
2. If Chautara calls someone then they must start by claiming they they are "गरीब प्रभर" or Poor.
3. King's Officers and Relatives must be addressed "साहेब" or Respected Sire.
4. If the King is seated on the throne, then One or Two Salute was to be given.
5. The Chautara must salute the King before expressing any form of requests. The Brother of the King was made Chautara.
6. A Brahminic Teacher must be addressed by the King himself.

7. In the *Kachahari* or *Bhardari Sabha,* one cannot flaunt their moustache, one cannot fold their legs.
8. The King should have Chautara besides him, his teacher on the right, Kaji or Minister seated with respect on the right side.
9. Brahmins, *Khas Kshetriya, Magar* and other elderly should request permission to be seated and seat likewise in their respective areas of the Assembly.

On Measurement
The Official Means of Measurement was:

- 10 Muthi=1 Mana
- 8 Mana= 1 Pathi
- 20 Pathi= 1 Muri

The Official Means of Measurement was:

- 10 Lal= 1 Masa
- 10 Masa=1 Tola - 18 Laal= 1 Pal
- 27 Tola= 1 Bodi
- 108 Tola= 1 Bisauli
- 2 Bisauli= 1 Dharni

On Loan and Interest

1. Interest cannot be received for after 10 years.
2. Interest Rate should be fixed to 20% for Food Borrowing.
3. This rule is applicable for Food Consumption Loan only.
4. Simply, after 10 years one can only take Thrice the amount they provided for.

5. On Money Loan, 10 % was the interest for 10 years. Hence, Double the money of what had been provided was the limitation.

On Minor Rules and Regulations

1. First Come and First Served regulations for Water and Oil.
2. These matters should be solved by the Local Panchayat's not the Royal Court.
3. Irrigation Tunnel could be made according to the Land Topography.
4. Water for Irrigation Purposes was to be divided systematically and in turns.

On The Six Houses of Gorkha

House Pandey, House Panta, House Aryal, House Khanal, House Rana Magar and House Bohara formed the Six Houses of Gorkha.

1. Ram Shah provisioned that among these six houses, Chautara, Kaji and Sardar should be elected or selected.
2. If any one of them plots against the crown or is disloyal to the crown in any form, then the King should be informed as fast as possible.
3. The Shah's should without any compromise never demote them and always provide the highest of ranks to these six houses.
4. The Six Houses are provided with the right to exercise Justice which is equal for all.
5. Bhattarai's were Ganesh, Khanal were Brahmins and Acharya's were Hotu in Karmakanda's and other Rituals.

6. Pandey, Panta and Aryal were treasurers. Three Magar's were Kapardari's. Dharmadikari, Sardar and Bhanse were also Aryal's

7. House Mishra was made the Royal Teacher or Priests by Ram Shah. They taught politics, Dharma Shastra's and so on.

8. House Aryal was made the Enforcers of Dharma or Laws known as Dharmadhikari.

On Forest Conservation

1. Cow should be grazed in Farmlands only.
2. Trees should be afforested in both sides of the road for resting and environment purposes.
3. If trees do not exist, then Landslide shall occur and Houses without Trees have no importance.
4. Those who cut trees present near houses should be fined Rs. 5.

On Punishment (Extracted from the 15th Thithi)

1. If the *Chautaria,* brothers and *Gotia* commit a heinous crime against the human body, expel them from the country upon razing their hairs on the head.
2. If the *Sanyasi, Bairagi* and *Bhat* commit similar crime banish them accordingly.
3. If you banish accordingly-in one hand you shall not be blamed for *Gotrahatya* (murder of the close relatives) and on the other hand nobody will raise finger against you for not punishing your close relatives-such a statement is found in the *Sastra* (Religious books) also. Hence, banishment is equal to the death penalty.

4. To execute a *Brahmin* may be blameworthy to *Brahmanhatya* (murder of a *Brahamin*), and if you do not execute them the others may blame you for impunity, therfore, *Mudnu* (razing hairs from someone's head) is equal to the death penalty, therefore banishment after razing the hair on head is the appropriate punishment.

5. *Bairagi, Sanyasi* and *Bhat* are un-executable; therefore, the appropriate punishment for them is banishment.

6. A female, likewise should not be executed or killed by any means, no matter how heinous the crime is.

7. Among Khas, Magar, Newar, only those who commit crime should be punished. Their family should not be punished. Hence, *Jasko Paap Usko Gardan* was proposed by Ram Shah.

Others:

1. Only Queen could wear Golden Ornaments or any form of décor. Those outside of the Royal Family had to ask permission to the King or the Queen to fulfill such demands. This law was installed by King Jayastithi Malla in Nepal and adopted by Ram Shah in Gorkha.

The Legal Procedure of Ram Shah

1. Ram Shah was the Chief Dharmadhikari of Dharmadhikaran. Hw was seated on Nyayasan for providing Justice. He seated himself with able brahmins and Ministers. The King should listen to both sides and provide a just decision based on it. It was based on Shukra Niti according to Dhundiraj Bhandari.

2. Educated Officers of Court were kept to form written complaints in the form. Bintipatra, Ijhar and Firadpatra were the three general types of such complaints.

3. After that, one had to sign or provide consent to the written complaint while mentioning Witness or Evidence of any kind.

4. If the requirements were met, then court would move on with the case.

5. The Alleged Criminal would be called by the soldiers of King for the case.

6. If the alleged was busy then, one could send their representative for simple cases. The Representative or Court could not be blamed if the alleged lost the case or was harmed in any way.

7. The representative would be paid 16% of the case worth. Representative could be kept in Civil cases only.

8. Cases of Criminal nature such as Murder or Killing, Theft, Kidnapping of Unmarried Girls, Defamation, Treason and Organ Deformation didn't have the provision of keeping representative.

9. If any of the parties of the case died in any way, then their children could either continue the case else it would be continued.

10. 'A case could be justly decided if Consistent and Clear Investigation of Evidence is conducted' was the principle.

11. Before any decision is made, the nature of the crime, the mens rea of Criminal, the age, occupation, power, money etc. of the criminal should be examined.

12. Decision doesn't equate to Justice. Justice is felt by the society not the court.

13. "Shastra haraye Kashi janu, Nyaya haraye Gorkha Janu"

Conclusion on Ram Shah

Ram Shah is proclaimed as the Just King in Nepal. He is said to have reformed sociolegal system in Gorkha. His

Judicial Administration is not yet known as vividly. His laws specially on measurement and Criminal Cases are practiced even to this day. Eg: Potato is weighed not on Kilograms but on Dharni. Simply, Ram Shah certainly introduced quite the legal reforms, but was highly limited to Gorkha itself. Even P.N. Shah's Legal Reform are limited to Gorkha as he conquered Nepal 26 years after he became King.

Dibya Upadesh By King P.N. Shah Introduction

Dibya Upadesh is the collection of Teachings expressed by Prithvi Narayan Shah at the outset of his life after he became the First King of Modern Nepal. Dibya Upadesh is translated to best or heavenly advice or Education. The Purpose of Dibya Upadesh was to deliver important Knowledge to the upcoming Generation and make them realize the importance of the Country.

Features of Dibya Upadesh

1. Nepal is like a Yam between Two Stones. So, Nepal needs to maintain good relations with Both the Stones i.e., India and China.

- "Whereas, this state (Nepal) is like a yam (gourd) between two stones. Keep strong friendship with the Emperor of China; one has to maintain friendship with the Emperor of the sea (English Emperor) in the south."

2. One should never be offensive in the attack especially if one is weak. The

True Strategist will always will through Defensive Tactics and attacking only when the time is right.

3. Prithvi Narayan Shah has expressed that Means of Persuasion, Manipulation, Various Tactics including Deceit is necessary in Politics and Diplomacy, especially in War.

4. A nation shouldn't endorse or accept or even practice Foreign Cultures and their way of Life. One

should buy only necessary Goods from them and do not buy excess from them.

"Export our products and other Herbs to the foreign countries and earn cash out of such commodities. Always try to earn money from external trade."

5. The Civil Servants selected by the Government must be loyal and should never betray you. They should also be honest and supportive.

6. The state of *Lamjung* is like Garud (an eagle); Gorkha is like a snake; Nepal is like a frog. Therefore, the snake has to manage the eagle at the outset then only snake can eat the

Frog. Prithvi Narayan Shah has provided the tactics to Warfare.

7. "I wanted to create a marriage bond between *Pandey* and Basnayat (particular castes). I advised to marry his (Mr. Kalu Pandey) daughter with Mr. Keher Singh, son of Mr. Shiva Ram Basnet. I arranged for a traditional marriage accordingly. After this bond between them we attacked Nepal with the shield(*Dhal*) of Pandey and sword of Basnayat."

8. Prithvi Narayan Shah used marriage as a Tool of Diplomacy and Unity rather than the expression of Love.

Analysis of Dibya Upadesh

There are many aspects of Dibya Upadesh that are Modern and awe-inspiring. He believed that army should be recruited on the basis of Equality and Loyalty rather than Nepotism. He also believed in the military technique of Counter-Attack with respect for Preofessionalism. Prithvi Narayan Shah urges the citizens of Kathmandu to be active and energetic. He wanted to initiate Youth Mobilization and Cultural Development. He despised an Import Based Economy.

Administration of Shah Dynasty

Central Administration Positions

1. King: King was deemed the Most Powerful Authority in Shah Dynasty

2. Regent: Many Kings of Shah Dynasty ruled with Regent's. They were too young to rule. So, Regents were major part of Shah Administration.

3. Crown Prince: Crown Prince also assisted King in his administrative and Judicial Duties. They were, sometimes, given the post of Hajuriya General.

4. Mukhtiyar: Mukhtiyar was the primal authority after the King. The post of Mukhtiyar was given to the most powerful Man in the administration. Bhimsen Thapa was a famous Mukhtiyar.

5. Chautariya: Before the position of Mukhtiyar, Chautariya served as the Prime Minister or the major advisor of the King.

6. Kaji: Kaji's were provided the administrative duties of a certain territory by the King. There were Four Kaji's in Hierarchy.

7. Sardar: Sardar were Military and Administrative Men of High Positions after Kaji's. They were also four in number.

8. Kapardar: Kapardar were trusted with taking care of the Palace. They can be deemed similar to Butler.

9. Khajanchi: They managed the Finance and trusted by Kings. They also distributed salary and planned to save budget.

10.Dharmadhikari: Dharmadhikari was the Most Important Judicial Officer of the State; They made sure that the Dharma Shastra's were followed in Nepal.

11. Khardar: They assisted in meetings or assemblies or in other administrative offices. They did the job of Writers.

Organizations

1. Bhardari Sabha or The House of Lords: Assembly of the Aristocratic Families of Nepalese Court. They actively participated in Politics.

2. Cha Thar Ghar: They have been mentioned in Dibya Upadesh as well as 26

Thithi's. They were the backbone of Shah Administration as they were the most trusted families by the King with sworn Loyalty. They were provided important posts as well.

Other Forms of Organizations and Assemblies such as Baggi Bithak, Daftar Khana and Chevdel were also present.

Judicial Administration Positions

1. Dharmadhikari and Representatives of Dharmadhikari

Dharmadhikari's were handpicked from knowledgeable Brahmins. They advised the king on how Laws should be made and Executed. The Representatives of Dharmadhikari presided over the court outside of the Kathmandu valley.

2. Dittha

- Thakuri's were made Dittha. They were the most important officers of a Ditrict Court. They managed the

Judicial Administration as well as Security of that District. They acted like District Judges.

-Men from Known and Powerful Families were made Dittha's.

3. Bichari

- Bichari's were the evidence gatherer and examiner in the Courts. They could also adjudicate some cases.
- Magar's were kept Bichari because they were presumed to be innocent and Loyal.

4. Bahidar

- Bahidar also worked in District Court and managed many aspects of the Court and assisted Dittha in such management.

Courts and Organizations

1. Kotling: Kotling dealt with cases related to Houses, Land as well as other cases that were Civil in nature.
2. Ithachapali: Ithachapali was concerned with solving Large and Major Disputes as well as cases that were Criminal in nature.
3. Taksar Adda: Taksar Adda dealt with cases related to Money, Finance as well as Rape.
4. Dhansar Adda: Dhansar Adda was concerned with cases of Untouchability and Caste.

They were known as Sadar Adalats. Courts were supposed to consist of One Dittha, One Bichari, One Kharidar, One Major or General, One Jamdar, One Hawaldar, Two Amaldar and Twenty-Five Police Officers.

CHAPTER VI

Rana Regime

Rana Regime

Jung Bahadur Kunwar was awarded the title of "Rana" after his reign as Prime

Minister and Commander-in-Chief. Before the event, he was Jung Bahadur Kunwar.

Jung Bahadur was born in 1874 B.S. Ashar or 1817 C.E. The Father of Jung Bahadur was Balnarsingh Kunwar and the mother of Jung Bahadur was the daughter of Bhimsen Thapa's sister.

Rise of Jung Bahadur

Kot Parva

- On Jestha of 1902 B.S. Mathwar Singh Thapa was also assassinated and a Joint

Cabinet was formed under Phatte Jung Shah, Gagan Singh Khawas and Abhiman Singh Rana. Phatte Jung Shah discovered the affair of Gagan Singh Khawas and Rajyalaxmi.

-Gagan Singh Khawas was also mysteriously assassinated. Queen Rajyalaxmi poured Gangajal in the face of the dead Gagan Singh Khawas and promised to avenge the murderers.

-The Queen told Jung Bahadur to call an assembly of all Bhardars in Kot Palace for the investigation of the murder. Kishor Pande, a courtier of Pande Family was made the Prime Suspect. The Queen Rajyalaxmi ordered Kishor Pande to be killed.

- The King, Rajendra Bikram Shah exclaimed that a proper investigation would occur before killing anyone and left the palace. After hearing this, the Queen Rajyalaxmi grabbed a sword by her hand and started throwing a tantrum.
- Jung Bahadur Kunwar, his brothers and army killed Abhiman Singh Rana. The Sons of Phatte Jung Shah and Brothers of Jung Bahadur Kunwar commenced a contest, a fight of sorts against one another.
- The Son of Phatte Jung Shah was killed. He decided to complain it to the Queen. Jung Bahadur ordered his brothers to kill him. Phatte Jung Shah was also stabbed and died.
- Queen ordered the Killing of all the responsible Bhardars. The prime suspect had been laid down on Pande's hence, many Pande's were killed in the massacre. Major Political Players and Courtiers were all killed by The Kunwar Family.

According to an Estimate, 31 Lives were lost that day including 3 Chautariya's and 7 Kaji's. For the killing of more than 30 Courtiers, Kot Massascre is said to be one of the most notorious and bloodiest massacre in Nepalese History.

Bhandarkhal Parva

-Jung Bahadur Kunwar, who was born in 1874 B.S. rose suddenly to the top of Nepal's Power Hierarchy I 1903 B.S.

-The Queen proposed to Jung Bahadur that Surendra should be replaced and Ranendra, her son should be made the King of Nepal. Jung Bahadur Kunwar solemnly refused to take part in her plan.

- She had made Jung Bahadur the Mukhtiyar of Nepal and Jung Bahadur "stabbed her in the back" for her reinforcement.So, The Queen Rajyalaxmi decided to kill him.
- Queen Rajyalaxmi, with confidentiality, plotted for the assassination of Jung Bahadur Kunwar with the Basnet Family. She promised Birdhwaj Basnet the position of Prime Ministership if he killed Surendra, Upendra and Jung Bahadur.
- Every prominent Courtier, who survived Kot Massascre was invited to a celebration. The celebration which was organized in Bhandarkhal Garden was in disguise a plot of assassination.
- Jung Bahadur Kunwar would be served in food or in drink with poison.One of the men knew about the massacre that would take place in Bhandarkhal and decided to warn Jung Bahadur about it. Jung Bahadur went and killed everyone who were the part of the assassination.
- In total, 23 men were killed among which 15 were Basnets. Hence, Bhandarkhal Parva is also known as Basnet Parva.
- Rajya Laxmi and Rajendra Bikram Shah went to Kashi where Rajendra plotted many times to assassinate J.B.R.
- So, Jung Bahadur Kunwar sent 5-6 letters to King Rajendra threatening to make Surendra The King of Nepal if he wouldn't return. King Rajendra instead of agreeing to Jung Bahadur's demands decided to sent two

assassins to kill him.

- Jung Bahadur declared that King Rajendra Bikram Shah would be dethroned and Crown Prince Surendra would be made King. Surendra was officially made the King of Nepal with Top Salami.

Alau Parva

In 1904 B.S. Shrawan a camp was set by Rajendra Bikram Shah with 4000 men. Among the 4000 men, only 1600 were armed soldiers. The camp was set in present day Parsa in the place called Alau. The Army of Rajendra Bikram Shah was attacked in the night and defeated.

Rajendra Bikram Shah was brough to Nepal in 1904 Shrawan 14. The Incident of when Rajendra Bikram Shah tried to gain back Nepal with the help of 4000 men but failed is known as Alau Parva.

Rajendra Bikram Shah was imprisoned by Jung Bahadur Kunwar after coming back to Nepal. He died in 1938 B.S. Ashar 30 or 1881 C.E. July 14 after 34 years in Imprisonment.

After the Alau Parva, Jung Bahadur Kunwar was honored with the title of "Rana" through the Lalmohar of King Surendra in 1906 B.S. He retired from the post of

Prime Minister in 1913 B.S. and became "Shree Teen" of Kaski and Lamjung. He returned when his brother died. Jung Bahadur Rana ruled from 1903-1933 B.S. and died while he was at a hunting adventure.

He limited the post of Prime Minister to Rana Family and established a role of succession.

Successors of Jung Bahadur

Ranoddip Singh became the Prime Minister after the death of Jung Bahadur Rana. 38 Saal Parva and 42 Saal Parva took place in 1938 B.S. and 1942 B.S. that caused the demise of Prime Minister of Ranoddip Singh and Jagat Jung (Son of Jung Bahadur) and The Jung Family. The sons of Dhir Shumshers became the Official Prime Ministers of Nepal.

Bir Shumsher ruled as the Prime Minister of Nepal for 13 years. As Khadga Shumsher was removed from the succession, Dev Shumsher became the new Prime Minister of Nepal. Dev Shumsher was known among the Shumsher Brothers to be democratic in nature.

He wanted to make an assembly similar to Bhardari Sabha. He established the first newspaper print known as "Gorkha Patra" in 1859 B.S. He established an assembly for six whole hours. He increased institutions of Education. He also commenced a suggestion box and planned to provide the Knowledge of Foreign Affairs to citizens. He was abdicated and removed from the Post of Prime Minister.

Chandra Shumsher was the 5th Eldest Son of Dhir Shumsher. He was born in 1863 C.E. July 8 or 1920 B.S. He was highly educated and Oxford University had provided him the title of "Doctorate of Law". After the forced resignation of Dev Shumsher and and his exile to Dhankuta, Chandra Shumsher assumed complete power over Nepal and ruled over it for 29 whole years.

Role of Succession by Chandra Shumsher

In 1977 B.S. Chandra Shumsher started a new role of succession to promote his sons. Chandra Shumsher lacked bastard or illegitimate sons but his brothers had a lot of them. Thus, Chandra Shumsher divided the Ranas into three classes and arranged who would be Prime Minister in a likewise fashion.

1. A Class Rana: If a Child is born from a legitimate and traditional marriage with a female from the Same Class.

2. B Class Rana: If a Child is born from a legitimate and traditional marriage with a female from a Lower Class.
3. C Class Rana: If a child is born from an unmarried relation.

The Ability of Each Class
A Class: Prime Minister
C Class: Leiutinent or Colonel

As mentioned earlier, the sons of Chandra Shumsher were born from legitimate wives, so, the Role of Succession of his children favored the new Division created by Chandra Shumsher.

Chandra Shumsher was succeeded by Bhim Shumsher. Bhim Shumsher was succeeded by Juddha Shumsher. Juddha Shumsher ruled for 13 years in Nepal from 1989 B.S. to 2002 Mangsir 14. Many events occurred during his reign.

Juddha Shumsher was succeeded as Rana Prime Minister by Padma Shumsher. Padma Shumsher was neither strict nor liberal in nature. He was pressurized by the Biratnagar Jute Mill Strike to bring in Constitutional reforms in Nepal. He ordered a change in Law of Nepal and Government of Nepal Act, 2004 was written and nearly promulgated. He resigned after going to India. Mohan Shumsher became the Prime Minister of Nepal. He was the last Prime Minister of Nepal.

Causes of Downfall of Rana Regime

1. Political Causes: India had also become Independent and many Political Organizations were being formed against Rana Regime.

2. Economic Causes: Huge Income Inequality existed during the Rana Regime. This caused frustrations against the Rana Regime.

3. Social Causes: The People's Consciousness was also rising and Many Nepalese Soldiers who went to Second World War had observed changes throughout the World.

4. Internal Division of Rana Family: Chandra Shumsher's division of Rana Family into A Class, B Class and C Class also caused internal disputes. C Class Rana's financed political parties and Anti-Rana Movements.

5. Rana's also lacked International Recognition and Acceptance due to a Totalitarian Regime.

6. Activeness of King Tribhuvan with other Political Parties.

Movement of Democracy in Nepal

1. Makai Parva

A Subba from Kaushal Adda named Krishnalal Adhikari published a book named "मकैं को खेश्ग " or Makaiko Kheti. It was a top-notch satire to the Rana Regime by describing Rana's as Pests. "From 1903 B.S. Pests started infesting Maize in Nepal. There are two kinds of Insects that eat Maize. One is Red in color and the other is Black in color." He was imprisoned where he died.

2. Establishment of Prachanda Gorkha

In 1988 B.S. Prachanda Gorkha was established in Nepal as an Anti-Rana Organization under the leadership of Captain Khandaman Singh Basnet.They also conspired to kill every member of the Rana Family in the occasion of

Tihar. The major conspirers were imprisoned where they died.

3. Nepal Praja Parishad

Nepal Praja Parishad was the first party of Nepal formed under the chairmanship of

Tanka Prasad Acharya. A meeting was held in the House of Dharma Bhakta Mathema in 1993 B.S. Jestha 22 and the Praja Parishad was officially established.

After the formation of Nepal Praja Parishad, a full event of Pamphlet Distribution was conducted for 4 months. Nepal Praja Parishad was popularized but The Rana's were unable to catch the involved members. They were finally caught and imprisoned. Not only that, The Infamous Murder of Four Men also occurred after this. Shukraraj Shastri, Dharma Bhakta Mathema, Dasharath Chand and Gangalal Shrestha were hanged after the incident.

4. Formation of Political Parties

Nepali National Congress was formed. Tanka Prasad Acharya became the Chairman of Nepali National Congress. B.P. Koirala became the acting chairman of Nepali National Congress. Balchandra Sharma, Dilliraman Regmi etc were also given prominent posts in the party.

Under the leadership of Mahendra Bikram Shah and Surya Prasad Upadhyaya, Nepal Prajatantra Congress was established in 2005 B.S. Shrawan 1.

In 2006 B.S. Bhadra 30 under Pushpalal Shrestha, son of Gangalal Shrestha The Martyr, Manmohan Adhikari, Tulsilal Amatya and D.P. Adhikari, Nepal Communist Party was established in Nepal.

In 2006 B.S. Chaitra 27 Nepali Prajatantra Congress and Nepali National Congress merged and formed Nepali Congress.

5. Biratnagar Jute Mill Strike, Jayatu Sanskritam and other Events

The Movement of Democracy reached its highest point in 2007 B.S. An Armed

Movement took place, King Tribhuvan left his palace and ultimately The So-Called Delhi Agreement took place that brought democracy in Nepal ending the 104 years Rana Regime that begun with Jung Bahadur Rana.

Abdication of King Tribhuvan

17 members of the Royal Family escaped with King Tribhuvan to the Indian

Embassy but Grandson Gyanendra Shah was left. In Magsir 12, 2007 B.S. under the Bijaya Shumsher, The Diplomat son of Mohan Shumsher and Keshar Shumsher, a mediation team was sent to Delhi. The Mediation team met with fierce demands Nehru always acted as an mediator and the three parties i.e. Congress, Ranas and King never talked face to face in that meeting. Finally, the diplomatic conversations had been completed and a final agreement and changes were introduced in Nepal including the End of Rana Regime.

Meanwhile, Nepali Congress had led an Armed Revolt that was successful with capturing of Biratnagar, Birgunj, most of the Eastern Districts and South-West Districts of Nepal. It was halted after the success of Negotiation going on in Delhi.

The Major changes introduced by the Nehru Mediated Meeting are:

1. Establish King Tribhuvan as King
2. Election for a Constituent Assembly
3. 14 Ministerial Cabinet with 7 for Ranas and 7 for People's Representatives

4. Freedom for all Political Prisoners

Thus, in Poush 26 2007 B.S. a message was sent by King Tribhuvan to the citizens of Nepal to end the revolution. He came to Nepal and declared that Rana Regime had ended and Democracy had arrived in Nepal. This was how Nepal Regime ended in Nepal.

Administration of Rana Regime

The Administration during Rana Regime was much managed although the posts were given to relatives. There were various Adda's that were distributed and had their own Jurisdiction. The Judicial Administration of Rana Regime was also much decentralized.

Administrative Positions

1. King: The King had minimal to no Power at all. They signed Acts, Laws and Decrees. They also had to proclaim the decisions made by the Prime Minister.
2. Prime Minister: The Rana Prime Minister were the De-Facto rulers of Nepal with near-absolute Power. They had complete control over Legislature, Executive and Judiciary. They had their Central Office known as Khadga Nisana Adda.
3. Commander-In-Chief: The Commander in Chief of Army was the next in role of Succession for The Post of Prime Minister. They were known as Mukhtiyar in earlier times. They dealt with appointing Governmental and Military Officers. They had control over various administrative offices.
4. West Commander General: The West Commander General exercised significant Power over the Western

Regions of Nepal. It was one step below the hierarchy of Commander-In-Chief.

5. Badahakim: Badahakim were kept in Large Cities outside of Kathmandu Valley. There were the Administrative Chief of those Areas. Palpa, Biratnagar, Birgunj etc. had Badahakims.

Others

1. Chautariya: Chautariya belonged to the Royal Family or held a Royal Lineage. They were provided with Administrative Power and made important decisions. 2. Kaji: Kaji's generally belonged to Aristocratic or Feudal Families. They were given control of Certain Territories.

3. Khajanchi: Khajanchu dealt with Financial Aspect of Nepal. They also managed the Treasury. Highly Trusted Personnels were only kept Khajanchi.
4. Sardar: Sardar's are lower in posting than Kaji but hold important power in Military and Administration.
5. Dittha: Dittha is comparable to District Judge or Chief Judicial Officer of a

District.

6. Mukhiya: Mukhiya were the administrators of a small territory or villages.
7. Bichari: Bichari's worked as Evidence Gatherer's.

Administrative Offices

1. Khadga Nissan Adda: Khadga Nissan Adda was established by Chandra Shumsher in 1974 B.S. This was the Office of The Prime Minister.

2. Bintipatra Niksari Adda: It is the highest Level of Office where requests are made regarding a certain event or Post. It is also called by some as The Highest Court of Review.
3. Muluki Adda: Muluki Adda is also known as the Office of Home Administration. This Office was the prime Administration Office of Nepal.
4. Jungi Adda: Jungi Adda was the Center of Military Administration and Management.
5. Muluki Khana: Nepal also had an Office for Revenue Collection and Review. It is known as Muluki Khana.
6. Bhandarkhal Dhukuti: This Office was located in Bhandarkhal where the treasury was kept. The Treasury acted as a reserve to support Nepal during Economic

Crisis.

7. Munsikhana: It was established by P.N. Shah for Foreign Affairs.
8. Ainkhana: Ain Khana was a Legal Office where discussion for the making of New Laws and Amendement of Old Laws took place. It was similar to Kaushal Adda.
9. Dharma Kachahari: It was kept by Jung Bahadur Rana to secure the religiously oriented practice of Nepal.

Judicial Administration Courts
(The Courts were the same as Shah Dynasty.)

1. Kotling: Kotling dealt with cases related to Houses, Land as well as other cases that were Civil in nature.
2. Ithachapali: Ithachapali was concerned with solving Large and Major Disputes as well as cases that were

Criminal in nature.

3. Taksar Adda: Taksar Adda dealt with cases related to Money, Finance as well as Rape.

4. Dhansar Adda: Dhansar Adda was concerned with cases of Untouchability and Caste.

Evolution of Courts in Rana Regime The Initial Period (1903 B.S. to 1958 B.S.)

Kaushal or Bhardari Sabha was the most important makers of Law and the prime protectors of Law as well. Muluki Ain, 1910 was the basis for all decisions.

Kaushal Adda was followed by Sadar Adalats. Under the Sadar Adalats were Kotling, Itachapali, Taksar and Dhansar. Below these Courts were Provincial Courts known as Gauda's.

The Middle Period (1958 to 1989 B.S.)

The Middle Period was unique because Prime Minister was made the Final Decider, the Ultimate Judge of Justice.

Below The Prime Minister was Bintipatra Niksari Adda were people could request for the review of cases. Below the Bintipatra Niksari Adda was Sadar Adda's and Bhardari Sabha. They were important in deciding cases and making small laws. Below The Sadar Adda's were Gaudas. They were located in important locations throughout Nepal. The Major Gaudas were located in Ilam, Dhankuta, Palpa, Doti etc. Badahakim also acted as a dispenser of Justice.

Below the Gauda's were District Courts located in most of the Districts followed by nearly 50 Amini Courts.

The Final Period (1989 to 2007 B.S.)

The Prime Minister was the Ultimate Judge. Below him was Pradhan Nyayalaya. Pradhan Nyayalaya was the Official Central or Supreme Court of Nepal. Pradhan Nyayalaya was followed by Sadar Bhardari.

After Sadar Bhardari there were Apil Adda. They were formed in Dhankuta, Katuhawan, Butwal, Saptari, Naya Muluk, Palpa and Doti. Below these Apil Addas were Amini Courts.

Conclusion

After 2007 B.S. Rana Regime Ended and the entire Court Structure of Nepal was radically changed. Within the 104 years of Rana Regime, Official Courts were abundant in Nepal. Although the Justice given during the Rana Regime is mysterious, The Judicial Administration was well structured and Organized.

Muluki Ain, 1910 B.S.

Introduction

- Muluki Ain, 1910 B.S. was promulgated under the reign of Prime Minister Jung Bahadur Rana.

He became The Most Powerful Man of Nepal after the Lalmohar of 1906 B.S. from King Surendra. He became The Prime Minister, Commander-in-Chief and later "Shree Teen" of Nepal.

- Jung Bahadur Rana also visited Europe, being the first Nepali to do so.
- He is said to have observed and liked the idea of English Common Law and also the Napoleonic Code which was drafted 100 years ago.
- He understood that having a National Law to govern the whole Country was necessary for International Recognition and Acceptance.
- He made a huge drafting committee of 221 Officials. He made Dharmashastra's the main basis of his Code. Hence, Muluki Ain, 1910 B.S. was put to practice.

The Hierarchy of Castes

There are the Five Hierarchy of Castes in the Muluki Ain, 1910. They were provided different Treatment by the Society and Government. The Punishment for the Crimes were also different.

1. The Uppermost in this Hierarchy lie Tagadhari's. They were Sacred Thread or Janai. Generally, Brahmins, Chetri's belong in this Class. Brahmins and Chetri's are not separated in this Hierarchy.
2. Below Tagadhari lie Matawali. They are from Mongoloid Race and have different facial structure than Aryans. They are said to be Alcohol Drinking and hence separated.
3. Choi Chito Halnu Naparne are those People who neither belong to the lowest class not to the highest Class. They are acceptable and one should purify themselves after touching or dealing with them. Foreigners fall under this class.
4. Choi Chito Halnu Parne are those People after who's contact one must purify themselves. They are Unacceptable and fall into The So-called Untouchables.

2. The Matters of Muluki Ain, 1910

- Muluki Ain, 1910 deals with Civil and Criminal Matters, Administrative Matters, Procedures, rules of Governance and conduct, Land Management, Revenue Administration, Land Survey as well as Division and Categorization of Lands.
- Muluki Ain also deals with Inter-Caste Marriage, Relation between Husband and Wife, Adoption, Partition of Property, Dowry, Inheritance etc.

- Muluki Ain, 1910 has provisions relating to Illicit Sexual Intercourse, Adultery, Molestation, Incest, Rape, Infanticide etc. It has laid down laws against Verbal Abuse, Brawling, Physical Assault, Murder and Manslaughter.
- Muluki Ain has mentioned laws on Witchcraft, Forced Labor etc.

Interesting Provisions

- Prime Minister has been given the right to dethrone the King under special circumstances.
- Misinterepretation and Negative Promotion of Muluki Ain, 1910 shall be punished.

Killing of Brahmins

- All other Caste except Brahmins are provided with Death Penalty. Brahma Hatya or killing of Brahmins is one of the Five Heinous Crimes or Panchamahapatak.

Hence, Brahmins aren't killed.

There is one exception to this rule. If a Brahmin kills an enthroned King then Brahmins are also provided with Death Penalty.

Civil Law

Marriage

- One can Marry a man or woman that has generational gap of Seven Generations.
- One can also marry the sister of their Wife.
- One can also marry the daughter of Maternal Uncle who is above 12 years.

- One can abduct a girl above 12 years with Consent
- A female who is above 14 years can deny marriage proposal.

Adoption
Priority

- Child of the Nearest Relatives - Else, Child of the Same Clan - Else, Child of The Streets - Else, Child allowed by Court

Requirements

- Adoption isn't allowed if any of the wives has a child. The Wife also cannot adopt if her husband has a child through other Wives.

Partition

- The property shall be partitioned according to the decision and will of The Parents. If Mother is alive then Property cannot be Partitioned.
- If Husband leaves the family then a share of his property should be provided to the Wife as Living Expenses.
- Widow is entitled to Property. If she turns out to be unfaithful then she shouldn't be provided Property. A Widow cannot sell her Property until she reaches the age of 45 years.

If someone dies without children then the Property is transferred to Brothers.

Other Provision of Civil Laws

- Muluki Ain, 1910 has the Provision of Dharmadhikari who shall act as a Judge. He shall decide cases and if laws have been violated or not. They are Religious Judges.
- One shall have to pay the fine of Rs. 10 for Gambling.
- One shall have to pay the fine of Rs. 100 for Gambling

Criminal Law

- Muluki Ain, 1910 has provisioned that matters relating to Incest, Enslavement, Sexual Intercourse, Caste and other issues in Madhesh Region can be dealt in Madhesh itself according to prevailing practices.

On Adultery and Sexual Intercourse

- Adultery has been made Punishable. If one commits adultery with the Wife of Husband who is abroad, then they shall be punished.
- If The Enslavable caste commit adultery, then they shall be killed
- If Illicit and Forced Sexual Conducts have been done to a married woman, widow, unmarried woman under 11 years then it is Punishable.
- The person who shall commit infanticide shall be punished with imprisonment for Six years.
- Sexual Intercourse with Animals is also punishable.

Other Laws

- The person who shall commit infanticide shall be punished with imprisonment for Six years.
- The Killing of Cow shall be fined with either Rs. 1 or Rs. 100 or Rs. 60.

If Slaves are forced to eat Semen or Excrement then they will be freed.

Division of Land

- Muluki Ain, 1910 has divided Land Ownership under Raikar Land Tenure System, Jagir Land Tenure System and Birta Land Ownership. These forms of Land Ownership are provided to the Citizens or Preferred Person By The King or Prime Minister.

Types of Courts

- Kausal Adda: The Supreme Legislative Body of The State where State Laws are made.
- Sadar Courts: It consists of Kotling, Ithachapali, Dhansar and Taksar Adda. They deal with Civil and Criminal Matters
- Gaunda Court: They are located in Major Areas of Nepal where The Office of Badahakim doesn't exist. It is aimed to provide Justice to citizens throughout Nepal.

CHAPTER VII

Constitutional History of Nepal

Constitutional History of Nepal

What is Constitution?

A constitution is a set of fundamental legal-political rules that:

1. are binding on everyone in the state, including ordinary lawmaking institutions;
2. concern the structure and operation of the institutions of government, political principles and the rights of citizens;
3. are based on widespread public legitimacy;
4. are harder to change than ordinary laws
5. as a minimum, meet the internationally recognized criteria for a democratic system in terms of representation and human rights.

The Major Elements of a Constitution are: Organs of Government (Legislature, Executive and Judiciary), Separation of Power, Fundamental Rights, Sovereignty and Constitutional Powers, Constitutional Commissions and Structure of State.

Constitution in Nepal

In Nepal, there have been Seven Constitutions till date. Among the Seven, the first constitution remained unapplied. Six Constitutions were practiced in Nepal. These Constitutions were the result of political and structural changes in Nepal. The End of Rana Regime, The End of Panchayat and The End of Monarchy all produced New Constitutions in Nepal. These are also known as the Apex or Supreme Law of the Land. The Seven Constitutions of Nepal are:

1. Government of Nepal Act, 2004
2. Interim Government of Nepal Act, 2007
3. Constitution of Kingdom of Nepal, 2015
4. Constitution of Nepal, 2019
5. Constitution of Kingdom of Nepal, 2047
6. Interim Constitution of Nepal, 2063
7. Constitution of Nepal

Government of Nepal Act, 2004

Background

The Government of Nepal Act, 2004 is the First Written Constitution of Nepal. It was announced during the Rana Regime when Padma Shumsher was the Prime Minister of Nepal.

Reason for Formation of Constitution

The Major Reason for the Promulgation of Government of Nepal Act, 2004 is the Biratnagar Jute Mill Strike conducted by Nepali National Congress. The Major Leaders of this Strike were arrested including B.P. Koirala. Nation-wide

Protest could be observed. So, Padma Shumsher announced that Legal and Constitutional Reforms will be brought to Nepal.

For the Formation of Constitution, a committee was brought under Shree Prakash Gupta from India. The Constitution was finished by 2004 B.S. Magh 13. After 25 days of the completion of Constitution, Padma Shumsher was sent to India for Medical Purposes and sent a letter of resignation from India. After Padma, Mohan Shumsher became P.M. of Nepal. He never promulgated the Government of Nepal Act, 2004.

Features of Government of Nepal Act, 2004

1. It consisted of 6 Parts, 68 Articles and 1 Schedule.
2. It was the First Written and Codified Constitution of Nepal.
3. Guaranteed The Future of Rana Prime Minister's

- Article 3 states that King and Prime Minister will continue according to the Role of Succession. Both The King and Prime Minister will enjoy power according to their historical practices.

4. Absolute Power to Rana Prime Minister

- Legislative, Executive and Judicial Power was vested on the Prime Minister (Rana's).
- Prime Minister could suspend the Constitution and the Law for Six Months. He had the Right to Emergency Power.

5. Bicameral Legislature

- Upper House would consist of 20-30 members selected by the Prime Minister.
- Lower House would consist of 70 members. 42 of those members would be selected by Election. 28 of those members would be selected by the Prime Minister.
- Among the 42 Members, 32 would be District Pradhan Panchas, 4 would be Metropolitan Pradhan Panchas of Four Major Cities, 2 would be from an Educated Class and 1 member each would be from Business, Birtawal, Feudal Lord, Government Officer, Labor Class and Aristocrat. The total becomes 42.
- Both Upper House and Lower House was Permanent. One Fourth of the Members would be removed every year in the Cycle of Four Years.
- The Legislature couldn't Promulgate Laws that changes the Original and

Traditional Power and Position of King and Prime Minister according to Article 34.

6. Fundamental Rights

- The Rights provided by Constitution of Nepal are regarding Personal Freedom, Freedom of Speech and Publication, Right to Assembly, Religious Freedom, Equality before Law, Right to Justice, Free Primary Education and Right to Vote.

7. Judiciary (Pradhan Nyayalaya)

- It had the provision for One Chief Justice and 12 other Judges.
- Prime Minister could remove and appoint Judges of Supreme Court.
- Lack of Independent Judiciary.

8. Panchayat System

- Three Tiers of Panchayat System: Village or Town, District and Lower House.
- This System was practiced in Nepal only and was Unique to Nepal.

Conclusion

Government of Nepal Act, 2004 was provisioned to continue Rana Regime in Nepal. It lacked the provision of Independent Judiciary, Proper Separation of Power and Rights relating to Justice. It was much progressive than Muluki Ain, 1910.

Interim Government of Nepal Act, 2007 Background

Interim Government of Nepal Act, 2007 was the result of the End of Rana Regime in Nepal and establishment of Democracy in 2007 B.S. Falgun 7. The End of Rana Regime guaranteed a Constituent Assembly elected by the People for the making of a new Constitution. For a Temporary Time, Rana-Congress Cabinet was running Nepal and this Constitution was promulgated.

Interim Government of Nepal Act, 2007 was promulgated in 2007 B.S. Chaitra 29.

Features of Interim Government of Nepal Act, 2007

1. It consists of Seven Parts, 73 Articles and 1 Schedule.
2. It was the first applied Democratic Constitution of Nepal.
3. Fundamental Rights

- Part 2 from Article 2-20 consists of Directive Principles of State and Fundamental Rights of Nepali Citizens.
- It guarantees rights including Rights of Citizens, Property of Community, No Forceful Nationalization, Equal Salary to Male and Female, No Exploitation, Social Security, Right to Labor and Cultural Rights.
- Article 12 mentions about International Peace and Foreign Policy.
- It guarantees Exclusive set of Fundamental Rights including Governmental Equality, Religious Freedom etc.

4. Constitutional Commissions

It mentions the presence of three Constitutional Commission including Auditor General, Public Service Commission and Election Commission.

5. Executive

- Part 3 from Article 21-27 mentions about the Executive.
- The King and Council of Ministers have been provided with Executive Rights and Powers. Article 21 provides exclusive rights of Army to the King.
- The Cabinet and the King had the ability to amend the decision of Judiciary.

6. Legislature

The Legislative Power have been vested on the King including the Rights to Amendment.

7. Judiciary

- Judiciary has been primarily mentioned in Part 3 Article 30-32 of Interim Government of Nepal Act, 2007. It has attempted to guarantee an Independent Judiciary.
- The Chief Justice and Other Judges will be appointed by the King of the recommendation of Council of Ministers.
- Pradhan Nyayalaya has been made the Court of Record.

8. Temporary Constitution which guaranteed Constituent Assembly.

Conclusion

Interim Government of Nepal Act, 2007 is quite democratic in nature. It guarantees division of Power between The King and Council of Ministers. It was temporary in nature and hence there was no Legislture in hand. It had guaranteed the formation of Constituent Assembly.

Constitution of Kingdom of Nepal, 2015

Background

This Constitution was made under the Leadership of the King (King Mahendra). The King had formed a Constitutional Commission under Shree Bhagavati Prasad Singh and 5 members. Sir Ivor Jennings was also brought as a Constitutional Expert. The King had denied the first two draft of the Constitution and agreed with the Third Draft.

Features of Constitution of Kingdom of Nepal, 2015

1. It consisted of 10 Parts and 77 Articles.
2. All Residuary as well as Discretionary Powers were provided to the King. The Emergency Power was also vested on the King.
3. Fundamental Rights

- Part 3 Article 3-9 consisted of Fundamental Rights. Rights relating to Personal Freedom, Equality, Property, Political Freedom were given. It ensured No Discrimination in Government on the basis of Caste, Class, Gender, Sex etc.
- Right to Constitutional Remedy was introduced for the first time by this Constitution. It meant that Writ Petitions could be issued in the Courts.

4. Executive
- The Executive Power was vested on the King. He could exercise it through the Council of Ministers. The King was given discretionary power over it.

5. Bicameral Legislature

- Nepal was based on Parliamentary System of Government. There were Two Houses: The Upper House or Maha Sabha and House of Representatives
- The Upper House consisted of 36 members. It was a Permanent House and lasted for an Unlimited Time. It ran through Single Transferable Vote System. 18 members were from the Kinga and the other 18 from House of Representatives.

- The House of Representatives were selected by the King through Adult Franchise. It was temporary and lasted for 5 years. It consisted of 109 members that were elected through First-Past the Post electoral System.

6. Constitutional Commissions

- It provisioned for Public Service Commission, Election Commission, Auditor General as well as Area Division Commission.
- The Chief Commissioners could serve for 5 years.

7. National Council
- This Constitution provisioned for a National Council similar to Privy Council of Britain.
The members of National Council were selected by the King and remained until the wish of the King.
8. Cabinet and Government

- It provisioned for a maximum of 14 Ministerial Cabinet.
- This Cabinet of Ministers had to be responsible to the Legislature.
- The King had been provided the Power to suspend the Cabinet of Ministers for a year and Start Direct Rule.

9. Supremacy of King

- This Constitution, directly or indirectly, provided a lot of Power to the King.
- The King had been granted Legislative, Executive, Judicial as well as Emergency Power.
- The King had Supreme Command over the Military as well.

10. Judiciary

- Similar to Interim Government of Nepal Act, 2007
- New Provisions were included in Supreme Court Act, 2013.

Conclusion

Constitution of Kingdom of Nepal, 2015 was heavily favored towards the King. It also introduced Parliamentary form of Government in Nepal. It also had some minor provisions of the Independence of Judiciary. It guaranteed a Bicameral Legislature and built the foundations of Current Constitution of Nepal. Important Fundamental Rights were also mentioned in this Constitution.

Constitution of Nepal, 2019

Background

King Mahendra took absolute Powers in his hand in 2017 B.S. Poush 1. He declared the beginning of Partyless-Panchayat System in 2017 Poush 22. Also, "Nepal Special Provisions Act, 2017" was under use for a temporary time.

The Constitution of Nepal, 2019 was formed under the leadership of Rishikesh Shah and six other members. They researched Panchayat practices of Nepal and India. On 2019 Poush 1, Constitution of Nepal, 2019 was promulgated by the King with Panchayati Practices.

This Constitution Promoted three Major Aspects: a.

Party less Panchayat System.

a. Return to Village National Campaign
b. 60% Vote Required to be The Leader of Panchayat Assembly.

Features of Constitution of Nepal, 2019

1. It consisted of 20 Parts, 97 Articles and 6 Schedules.
2. It was applied for 26 years with a total of 3 Amendments. It is the longest practiced Constitution of Nepal.
3. It promoted Nationalism. It had provisioned for Nepalese Citizenship on Part 2 with various requirements and rights regarding Citizenship.
4. Fundamental Rights

- Part 3 Article 10-16 mentions Seven Fundamental Rights. It includes Right to Equality, Right to Freedom, right against Exile, right against Exploitation, Right to Religion and Property. Finally, Right to Constitutional Remedy was also included.

5. Fundamental Duties
- The Constitution also provisioned for Four Fundamental Duties. a.
Be Loyal towards the Kingdom of Nepal.

b. Respect Law and exercise Individual Rights without hindering rights of others
c. Follow the Government and National System according to the Constitution.
d. Do not Hinder the Sovereignty and Infallibility of Law.
- Directive Principles of Panchayat were mentioned in

Article 19.

6. Absolute Monarchy

- The Sovereignty of Nepal was vested on Nepal.
- Executive, Legislative and Judicial Powers were vested on the King.

He was the Supreme Commander of Nepal Army, The Head of State and The Head of Government.

7. Judiciary

- Supreme Court was mentioned in Article 68. It was the Court of Record.
- The Judges of Supreme Court had appointment limited to 65 years of age.
- Certain Requirements had to be met including 10+ years of Experience as a Legal Practioneer and so on.
- Ordinary and Extra-Ordinary Jurisdiction was provided to the Supreme Court.
- Judicial Committee was also provisioned.

8. Constitutional Commissions

- Election Commission, Public Service Commission, Auditor General, Attorney General and Commission for the Investigation of Abuse of Authority were provisioned by the Constitution.

9. National Panchayat

- Multi-Party Politics was banned in Nepal.
- There were Four Tiers of Panchayat according to the Constitution. Village or Town Panchayat, District Panchayat, Zonal Panchayat and National Panchayat.

- The National Panchayat was formed from 112 Members. It included members of Each District. They were elected every five Years.
- ¼ or 28 members of the National Panchayat was elected by the King.
- Seven Special Rights were provided to the National Panchayat.

10. Cabinet of Ministers

- At least 60% Majority from the National Panchayat was required to be the Leader of the Cabinet of Ministers.
- If No one was able to command 60% Majority then Three Most Vote Commanding Names had to be sent to the King. The King would select one of them from the three.

Conclusion

Constitution of Nepal, 2019 was the result of Party less Panchayat System with Absolute Power to the King. It restricted any form of Political or Democratic Practices. It provided few numbers of Rights to the Citizens of Nepal. The Constitution doesn't feature the required Independence of Judiciary and lacks in many circumstances. It is also called "The Nepal-Favorable Constitution" by many.

Constitution of Kingdom of Nepal, 2047

Background

In the Leadership of The Supreme Commander Ganeshman Singh, People's Movement I was successfully completed. It restored Multi-Party Politics and ended Party less Panchayat in Nepal.

Under the Leadership of Biswonath Upadhyaya, a seven membered Constitutional Improvement Council was formed. Later, a new Constitutional Drafting Committee was formed under Biswonath Upadhyaya again. The Committee submitted the draft of the Constitution. The Draft was named Constitution of Kingdom of Nepal, 2047 was also accepted in 2047 B.S. Karthik 23. The Constitution was mutually agreed upon by King, Congress and The Communists.

Some Argue that the Constitution is Fully Democratic. Others say it is a Black and Problematic Constitution made not by Assembly but by The Drafting Committee. Another Group provided it with Support as well as Critic.

Features of Constitution of Kingdom of Nepal, 2047

1. It consisted of 23 Parts, 133 Articles and 3 Schedules.
2. It vested the Sovereignty, not on the King but on the People. (Article 3)
3. Supreme Written Constitution.

- Article 1(1): This Constitution is the Fundamental Law of The Land

4. The Constitution has provisions related to Citizenship in Part 2 Article 8 to 10.

5. Fundamental Rights: Article 11 to Article 23.

It provides rights to Equality, Freedom, Publishing, Criminal Justice, Preventive Detention, Information, Property, Education and Culture, Religion, Right against Exploitation and Exile, Right to Privacy and Right to Constitutional Remedy.

- It also mentions Doctrines of Positive Discrimination, Right against SelfIncrimination, 24 hrs Rights and the Right to exercise 5 Writ Petitions.

6. Directive Principles and Policies of State.

- Part 4 Article 24-26 mentions about these Features.
- It has included 5 Directive Principles including the mention of Welfare State.
- It has mentioned 16 policies including Liberalization of Economy and Plans for Equality.

7. Constitution of Kingdom of Nepal, 2047 guaranteed Constitutional Monarchy in Nepal with Rule of Law and Constitutionalism.

8. Executive

- Article 35 has mentioned that "THE KING-IN-COUNCIL" method of Exercising Power will be followed. The Executive Powers would be shared by Council of Ministers and the King.
- An Executive could be formed through three ways: Complete Majority, Two or More Parties Majority and Members Majority.

9. Bicameral Legislature

- "THE KING-IN-PARLIAMENT" doctrine was followed.
- It provisioned for House of Representatives and National Assembly. They could change every law and decree except Universal Truth.
- The House of Representatives was the Lower House. It consisted of 205 members with at least one member from one District. They had the deadline of 5 years with one-year Extra-deadline. They could be a member of HoR at the age of 25 years.
- National Assembly was a Permanent House which consisted of 60 members. 10 of the members were selected by the King.

10. Independent Judiciary

- It provisioned for three level of Judicial Courts in Article 84.
- It mentioned that there should be one Chief Justice and 15 other Judges. They had the term of office till 65 years.
- Supreme Court was provided with both Ordinary and Extra-Ordinary Jurisdiction.
- Supreme Court was provided with the Power of Judicial Review making it a Powerful Organ.

11. Amendment

- It provisioned for the Amendment of Constitution in accordance with The Basic Structure Doctrine.

12. It also mentioned Major Constitutional Commissions, Political Parties and Emergency Powers.

Conclusion

This Constitution is regarded by many to be one of the most democratic Constitutions of the world. It includes many fundamental rights with Constitutional Remedy. It has, in theory, provided an Independent Judiciary. Doctrines of Constitutionalism and Rule of Law are clearly visible. Also, the Balance of Powers between the Parliament and King can be observed.

Interim Constitution of Nepal, 2063

Background

Interim Constitution of Nepal, 2063 is the Sixth Constitution of Nepal and the Second Interim Constitution of Nepal. This constitution was established after 19 days of People's Movement I in 2062/2063. Also, The Movement resulted due to the 12-Point Agreement between the Seven Political Parties and Maoist against the King.

The Constitution was completely drafted in 2063 B.S. Bhadra 9. The Interim Constitution of Nepal, 2063 was promulgated and applied in 2063 Magh, 1.

Features of Interim Constitution of Nepal, 2063

1. It consists of 25 Parts, 167 Articles and 4 Schedules.

2. It has vested Sovereignty on the People. It is also the First Constitution by the People to the People.

3. It proclaims that Nepal is a Federal Democratic Republican State.

4. Fundamental Rights

- The Constitution has guaranteed 21 fundamental Rights from Article 12 to Article 32.
- It also guaranteed several new Fundamental Rights. They are: Right against Untouchability, Right to Environment, Health, Employment, Female, Social Justice, Labor and Child.

5. Directive Principles and Policies
- It has mentioned 19 Directives, 6 Principles and 22 Policies to be adopted by Nepal.

6.   Ceremonial President and Vice-President
7.   Cabinet

- The Cabinet was to be formed with all of the members from Seven Political Parties.
- If the Cabinet was dissolved then 2/3 rd Majority would ensure a New Cabinet.
- Nearly 17 attempts were made at being the Prime Minister which failed.

8. Constituent Assembly that acted as Prime Minister

- For the first time before the election, there would be 330 members in the Legislative Assembly to prevent the hollowness of Legislation.
- After the Election of Constituent Assembly, 575 members would be selected from Election and 26 members from the Recommendation of Council of Ministers.

- Among the 575, 240 would be elected from First-Past-The-Post Electoral System and 335 would be selected from Proportional System.
- The Constituent Assembly were said to have the limit of 2 years with 6 months extra time.

9. Judiciary

- It provisioned for One Chief Justice with Fourteen other Judges
- It also mentioned about Judicial Council with Five Members for the recommendation of Judges.

10. Major Constitutional Commissions were included with National Human Rights Commission as well.
11. The Concept of Local-Self Governance was promoted.
12. National Security Council, Constitutional Council, Election Area Commission were also included in the Interim Constitution.
13. Referendum, Parliamentary Hearing, Emergency Powers are also mentioned with the provisions of Amendment of Constitution.

Conclusion

The Interim Constitution of Nepal, 2063 was promulgated to act as a guidance to The Constituent Assembly. It provisions for an Inclusive Constitution Making Process in Nepal. It promotes the concepts of Human Rights and Positive Discrimination as well as Social Justice. Hence, despite being for a Temporary Period, it was one of the most modern Constitutions of Nepal.

Constitution of Nepal

Background

A Constituent Assembly was established by the Interim Constitution to draft Nepal's temporary constitution, but due to disagreements, the Constituent Assembly postponed the promulgation of the new constitution by a year. After the most recent extension, the Constituent Assembly was dissolved for failing to complete the constitution.

An Election was held for the Second Time for the Constituent Assembly. Constitution of Nepal was finally promulgated in 2072 B.S. Ashoj 3.

Features of Constitution of Nepal

1. Written Constitution

Nepali constitution has 35 parts, 308 Articles, 9 Schedules and a preamble. The Constitution is declared as the Fundamental Law of the Land in Article 1(1).

2. Nepal as a Secular State

Nepal is an independent, indivisible, sovereign, secular, inclusive, democratic, socialism-oriented, federal democratic republican state with a constitution as the fundamental law. 3. Fundamental Rights

A total of 31 Fundamental Rights has been mentioned by the Constitution of Nepal in Part 3 from Article 16 - Article 46.

3. Three Layered Federalism

The main structure of Nepal consists of three levels: Federation, State and Local. There is One Federation, Seven

Provinces and 753 Local Levels. The constitution restructures Nepal as a federal country with three layers of federalism. The constitution provides separate list of powers for the federal layers, elaborate legislative and financial procedures for each level, and establishes a national natural resources and fiscal commission.

4. Executive

The executive power of Nepal is vested in the Council of Ministers, which is chaired by the Prime Minister. The Prime Minister shall command the Majority of The House of Representatives.

The prime minister is elected by the legislative-parliament based on majority. A no confidence motion against the prime minister must also come with a proposal for the new prime minister. Article 100 Mentions about the Vote of No-Confidence

5. Bicameral Legislature

The Legislature of Nepal was Bicameral. House of Representatives consists of 275 members among which 165 members are elected through FPTP and 110 through Proportional System. National Assembly consists of 59 members with eight members from Each Provinces through Single Transferable Vote System and 3 Recommended by Council of Ministers.

6. President

The president is constitutional head of the country and has the power to exercise his/her rights and duties as provided for by this constitution and federal laws. The president is also independent of the judiciary with the provision of Constitutional Bench.

7. Independent Judiciary

According to part 11, the Supreme Court will specialize on constitutional issues by creating provision for a constitutional bench. Five judges will be assigned to this bench. Further, constitutional council will nominate the chief justice and head and members of the constitutional commissions. The judicial council will nominate the judge of the supreme, high and district courts, the judicial system is an integrated one. - Provision of Constitutional Bench, Judicial Council etc. can be observed.

8. Emergency

If a grave emergency arises in regard to the sovereign territorial integrity of Nepal or the security of any part there of war, external aggression, armed rebellion, extreme economic disarray, natural calamity or epidemic, the president may declare or order a state of emergency in respect of the whole of Nepal or of any specified part thereof (Article 273).

Other Special Features of Nepal includes Constitutionalism, Rule of Law, Separation of Power and Check and Balance, Judicial Review etc.

Conclusion

The New Constitution of Nepal is committed to a multi-party democratic governance system, civil liberties, fundamental rights, human rights, adult franchise, periodic elections, complete press freedom, independent, impartial and competent judiciary and the concept of rule of law.

CHAPTER VIII

Post–Modern History of Nepal

2007-2017 B.S.

Political Events between 2007 to 2017 B.S.

After 2007 B.S. Multiparty democracy was practiced in Nepal under King Tribhuvan and King Mahendra. An Interim Cabinet was formed which included 5 Ministers from the Ranas and five ministers from Nepali Congress. The Prime Minister was Mohan Shumsher. B.P. Koirala was the Home Minister. After 9 months, B.P. Koirala resigned and the Cabinet was automatically dissolved in Karthik 26 2008 B.S.

Then, the First Government of Nepali Congress was formed under the leadership of Matrika Prasad Koirala, The Elder Brother of B.P. Koirala in 2008 B.S. Mangsir 1. Due to internal conflict within Nepali Congress, Matrika Koirala resigned in 2009 B.S. Shrawan 26.

After that, A Government was formed by King Tribhuvan under Keshar Shumsher which lasted till 2010 B.S. Ashad 2. Other Minor changes also happened. King Tribhuvan died in 2011 B.S. Chaitra 30. King Mahendra started a Direct Rule over Nepal. He also provided opportunities to Tanka Prasad Acharya, Dr. K.I. Singh as Government Prime Ministers. Mahendra again took direct powers in his hand until the Constitution of 2015 B.S. was declared.

King Mahendra declared an election for 2015 B.S. Falgun 7. Until then, a Government under Subarna

Shumsher was brought by King Mahendra.

The election took place and Nepali Congress won 74 seats and became the most powerful party of Nepal. B.P. Koirala became the first elected Prime Minister of Nepal. He formed a Cabinet in 2016 B.S. Jestha 13.

After One and Half Year in Poush 1st 2017 B.S., King Mahendra arrested all democratic leaders and begun his direct rule using Article 55 of the Constitution. In Poush 22nd 2017 B.S. he declared the beginning of Partyless Panchayat in Nepal with the following allegations:

1. Not adhering to National Duty and Responsibility
2. National Interest wasn't preserved.
3. Personal Benefits in the name of Democracy
4. Illegal and Unlawful Activities.

Thus, Unstable Politics, Tyranny and Disputes of the First Ten Years of Democracy were all swept away by King Mahendra.

Pradhan Nyayalaya Act, 2008 Introduction

Pradhan Nyayalaya was established by Juddha Shumsher in 1997 B.S. It was the highest level of Court but there was no specific law to tailor or guide it. Also, Justice Dispension was irregular and not fair. Hence, a new Law to deal with Judiciary, an organ of Government was necessary.

Pradhan Nyayalaya was promulgated and brought to use in Poush 8, 2009. It consists of 41 Sections.

Features of Pradhan Nyayalaya Act, 2008

1. Judges

- There is provision of One Chief Justice and Four Judges. The Tenure of the Judges shall be till the age of 65.
- The Judges shall be appointed by His Majesty and recommended by His Majesty's Government.
- Sec 8-10 argues that more than 10 years of Experience as a Judge and Lawyer should be required.

2. Some of the Important Provisions in Pradhan Nyayalaya Act are: Contempt of Court, Three Types of Benches, Power to Initiate and Transfer Cases, Provision of Case Law or Precedent and Ad Hoc Judge.

3.Pradhan Nyayalaya could initiate Five Types of Writs according to Section 30. It is Mandamus, Habeas Corpus, Certiorari, Prohibition and Quo-Warranto.

4. District Judge is appointed by King on the recommendation of Pradhan Nyayalaya.

Analysis

- Judicial Activism – Unitary Structure of Judiciary – Lack of Privacy due to Open Bench – Structural Dependence – Legal Formalism
- Hari Prasad Pradhan was the First Chief Justice of Nepal. H used Indian Courts as a Persuasive Source of Law. He also brought Interpretation of Statute Act, 2010 and Civil Rights Act, 2012.

Important Cases of Pradhan Nyayalaya

Bed Shrestha V. Secretary of Industry and Commerce

Pradhan Nyayalaya as Protector of Fundamental Rights
Provision of Dynamic Writ Petition
B.P. Koirala V. HMG
Right to Freedom of Citizens

Civil Rights Act, 2012 Introduction

Civil Right Act, 2012 can be understood as a sign, an emblem of Democratic Nepal. It was promulgated through the help of Hari Prasad Pradhan, The First Chief Justice of Nepal. Civil Rights Act, 2012 consists of the rights provided to the Citizens of Nepal. It is quite similar and resembles Fundamental Rights of Constitution.

Civil Rights Act consists of 22 Sections.

Features of Citizens' Rights Act, 2012

1. Equality Before Law

Section 3 of Civil Rights Act has guaranteed Equal Protection before Law. It states that "No citizen shall be denied equality before the law and equal protection of law subject to the provisions of prevailing laws."

2. Prevention of Discrimination

Section 4 guarantees Right against Discrimination. It has provided that individuals shall be selected on the basis of Merit.

3. Positive Discrimination

Civil Rights Act has ensured that Positive Discrimination, in some cases, shall happen to Children, Females and Minorities.

4. Rights in relation with Justice

It guarantees that one shall have the right against Double Jeopardy and SelfIncrimination.

5. File Cases against The Government

Section 18 states that one has Rights to Initiate Cases against HMG.

Other Rights Ensured by Civil Rights Act are as follows:

- Rights relating to Freedom on Section 6 - Rights relating to Religion on Section 7
- Rights relating to Property on Section 9
- Rights relating to Privacy on Section 10
- Rights against Child Exploitation on Section 14 etc.

State Cases Act, 2017 Introduction

State Cases Act consists of 11 Sections and 2 Indexes. It defines what a Government Attorney means. It also defines Court as the combination of Judges, Bench and Judicial Authority. It has also guaranteed the Universal Application of Law in Section 1.

Features of State Cases Act, 2017

1. Filing of Case

- Section 3 has mentioned that one can file a case that has Evidence. Then, one must report the case to the nearest Police Station with Written or Spoken Information.
- If there is no clear evidence, one can report the case to Police Station with sufficient suspicion. After that, Police Shall collect the required information of the case and see if it has evidence.

2. Investigation of a Case

- While Police are Investigating for Evidence, they cannot inflict any form of Punishment.
- If the Court Orders for Proper Investigation once again, Re-Investigation must be carried out.

3. Sec 4 mentions that a Civil Cases Investigation shall be underway after the Filling of Firadpatra with Appropriate Signatures.
4. Wrong Evidence

- Section 10 provides that if anyone gives Wrong Statement or Wrong Evidence of any king then, they will be punished according to Law. The Information given by the Alleged or whom case is filed against will also be considered.

5. Statute of Limitation

State Cases Act, 2017 has provisioned Myadthap or Hadmyad. According to the Act, if not mentioned then the Highest Statute of Limitation shall be 2 years.

6. Cases against the State

- Section 6 provides that if someone wants to file a case against the state then, the address of the Office of Employee should be addressed not the employee.

7. Government Attorney

Section 10 has mentioned rules to guide the services, requirement and duties of a Government Attorney.

(State Cases Act, 2017 was implemented on Baisakh 1 2018 B.S. and was repealed by Government Cases Act, 2017)

2017-2047 B.S.

Political Events from 2017-2047

After the Royal Coup of 2017 B.S. Partyless Panchayat System was applied in Nepal. Some of the Principles and Campaigns of Partyless Panchayat are:

1. Return to Village National Campaign
2. Politics for Development
3. All Nepalese Pancha, All Pancha Nepalese.
4. National Bonding and Brotherhood
5. National Mediation

Panchayat also introduced Land Reform Act, 2021 that had the objectives of Reasonable Distribution of Farmable Land and Improvement of Agricultural Productivity. It eradicated all forms of Land Tenure System except Guthi. It also planned on mobilizing Capitals kept in Lands. Thus, Kipat Land Tenure, Birta Land Tenure, Raikar Land Tenure ended.

National Referendum

The Arrested Leaders in 2017 B.S. were freed by 2025 B.S. They started living in India or lived secret lives in Nepal. King Mahendra died in 2028 B.S. Birendra became the King of Nepal in 2028 B.S.

In 2033 B.S., B.P. Koirala returned Nepal with the policy of National Mediation. He was immediately arrested. Also, a huge protest begun in 2035 B.S. against the Murder and Assassination of Many Political Leaders and Anti-Freedom Policy of Panchayat Government.

In 2035 B.S. Chaitra 22, Former Prime Minister of Pakistan Zulfikar Ali Bhutto was killed by the Present Prime Minister. Students of Nepal protested against it in The Pakistan Embassy. Nepal's National Police tried to silence the protesters. In response, the protest heated up. From 2036 B.S. Baisakh 10 most of the Campuses were closed.

King Birendra announced in 2036 B.S. Baisakh 10 a referendum to be conducted in 2037 B.S. Baisakh 20. 48 Lakhs Citizens participated in the National Referendum.

The Yellow Color stood for Reformed Panchayat which obtained 24.33 Lakhs votes.

The Blue Colour stood for Multiparty Democracy which obtained 20 Lakhs votes.

Politicians like B.P. Koirala, Manmohan Adhikari, Ganeshman Singh called it

Planned Propoganda. The Age of 18-21 years weren't allowed to vote in the Referendum.

Some of the Reforms after the National Referendum are:

1. Elections to be conducted every Five Years.
2. Person with 60% Majority in National Panchayat (Central Assembly) can be Prime Minister.

3. Rule of Law to be maintained between Executive and Legislative.

Many revolts such as Plane Abducation, Jhapa Revolt, The Satyagraha of 2042 etc. expressed Political dissatisfaction among the people throughout The Panchayat Regime.

Peoples Movement I

In 2046 B.S. the leading Parties of Nepal (Underground) decided to conduct a united peaceful protest against The Panchayat Regime. Meetings were conducted in the House of Ganeshman Singh. From 2046 B.S. Magh 5-7 meetings were held with nearly 3000+ representatives including famous Indian Politicians like Chandrasekhar, Harikishan Singh etc.

In Falgun 7 2047 B.S. Huge rallies were conducted in the Kathmandu Valley with Public Assemblies under the leadership of Ganeshman Singh. Protests heated in Chitwan, Bhaktapur and Dhanusa in Falgun 7, 8, 9 respectively. Similar programs and rallies were conducted throughout Nepal for 49 Days. Even Helicopter attacks were done against the protesters. In Chaitra 26 Evening 11:10 PM King Birendra declared that Partyless Panchayat had ended.

After the Peoples Movement an Interim Government under Krishna Prasad Bhattarai were called to the Government to conduct the elections successfully. 20 Parties took part in the 2047 Elections. 72 Lakhs+ Voters voted for 1345 Candidates. Nepali Congress gained majority and Girija Prasad Koirala successfully commanded the Majority.

Evidence Act, 2031 Introduction

Evidence Act, 2031 was the first Statutory law of Nepal to govern Evidence, the admittance of Evidence, Witness and other aspects of Evidence. It was promulgated on 2031 B.S. Poush 5. It consists of Nine Chapters and 56 Sections.

Features of Evidence Act, 2031

1. Burden of Proof
   - Section 25 states that The Burden of Proof that accused has committed the offense in civil or criminal cases lies on the Plaintiff. However, The Burden of CounterProof lies on the Defendant.

2. Provision of Estoppel

Chapter 5 has mentioned about Estoppel. It legally banns contradictory statements, evidences or other forms of Expressions.

3. Examination of Witness

Section 40-45 of Evidence Act discusses the Examination of Witness. Witness should be capable and Sane enough to accept the credibility of their evidence.

4. Expert Opinion

Section 23 expresses about Expert Opinion required on several kinds of Evidences.

5. Hearsay

- The Principle that Hearsay Evidence is No Evidence was highly appreciated.
- Hearsay Evidence were always taken up as Secondary Evidence and thus wasn't accepted.
- There are exceptions of Hearsay Evidence. Dead Person's Hearsay Evidence should be trusted according to the Court.

6. Relevant Fact

- Relevant Fact are those facts that decides a case and brings huge changes in the case. The Examination of Relevant Facts should be conducted according to the Evidence Act.

7. Presumption of Law and Presumption of Fact
8. Admission and Confession
9. Oral Evidence, Written Evidence, Physical Evidence etc.

2047-2072 B.S.

Political Events from 2047-2072 B.S.

Peoples Movement II

The Government of Girija Prasad Koirala implemented the policies of Globalization and Liberalization in Nepal making Nepal an Import Based Economy. He dissolved the Parliament and Mid Term Elections were held. CPN UML commanded the Government under Manmohan Adhikari in 2052 B.S. They started the Build Your Own Village Campaign and every Village Development Committee was provided 3 lakhs to do so. They were again removed and continuous Political Stability with the Maoist Uprising accompanied Nepal.

In 2058 Jestha 19, Narayanhiti Massacre took place that killed the entire Royal Family of Nepal. King Birendra, Queen Aishwarya, Prince Dipendra, Nirajan and Shruti all died. Dipendra became King for three days and died. It meant that King Gyanendra was the new King of Nepal.

In 2061 B.S. Magh 19 King Gyanendra started Direct Rule over Nepal. The Seven

Parties along with Maoist signed the 12 Point Agreement against the Direct Rule. In 2062 B.S. Chaitra 24 the parties begun Peoples Movement II. It lasted for 19 days and happened throughout Nepal. Girija Prasad Koirala acted as the leader of Peoples Movement II. In 2063 Baisakh 11 King Gyanendra said that I am returning to the People what is rightfully theirs ending the Peoples Movement. It is said that Nearly 50 Lakhs People took part in the Protest.

Constituent Assembly

After The Success of Peoples Movement II, a Council of Ministers was formed under Girija Prasad Koirala with members of all parties. In 2064 B.S. Jestha there was an agreement among the parties to conduct an election of Constituent Assemly. Interim Constitution of Nepal, 2063 was amended and the seats in the election was declared to be 601. 54 Parties participated in the election. Nearly 1 Crore 76 Lakhs citizens took part in the election with nearly 4000 candidates.

The First Constituent Assembly's election were completed with the term of 2 years to give a new Constitution to the People. It was extended again and again until 2069 B.S. Jestha when it was dissolved. Another election was conducted where Nepali Congress, CPN ULM and CPN Maoist won 196, 175 and 80 Seats respectively. Its term was extended again for 6 months after completion of 6 months. In 2072 Ashoj 3rd Constitution of Nepal was promulgated.

Constitution Making Process

1. Election of The Constituent Assembly
2. Establishment of Subject-Matter or Sectional Committees
3. Entries and Suggestions from Citizens and Professionals.
4. Preliminary drafts formed by the Sectional Committees
5. Brief discussions in the Constituent Assembly over the Initial Draft
6. Preparation of the Initial Draft of the Constitutiom
7. Editing and Restructuring Suggestions of Citizens and Members of CA into the Initial Draft.
8. Discussions of the Initial Draft of the Constitution and Acceptance of the Articles of the Constitution.
9. Nationwide Public Forums and debates on the Proposed Constitutional Draft
10. Creation of The Constitutional Bill and Adoption of Pertinent Recommendations
11. Debate in Constituent Assembly regarding Each Section with Consideration of

Amendments for The Bill's Approval

12. Final Approval by the Constituent Assembly

13. Signing of the Final Constitution by members of CA and certified by The Chair of Constituent Assembly.
14. Promulgation of the Constitution by The President
15. Application of The New Constitution and Arrangement of a new Election.

12 Point Agreement Introduction

12 Point Agreement was an agreement between Seven Parties of Nepal and Maoist to unite together. This agreement was done when King Gyanendra had taken Absolute Power in his Hands.

The Seven Parties and Their Leaders are:

- Nepali Congress: Girija Prasad Koirala
- CPN UML: Madhav Kumar Nepal
- Nepali Congress (Democratic): Gopal Shrestha
- Rastriya Janamorcha: Amik Sherchan
- Sadvabhana Party: Bharat Yadav
- Bammorcha: Krishna Shrestha
- Majdoor Kisaan Party: Prem Suwal

Features of 12 Point Agreement

1. It proposed the End of Absolute Monarchy through the establishment of Independent and Sovereign Nepal.
2. It aimed at vesting the Sovereignty on the People.
3. It also planned on the election of Constituent Assembly and Formation of Interim Government and Constitution.

4. The Maoist's declared that they would agree for Permanent Peace and join a Progressive Political Outlet.
5. Maoist promised to be institutionalized as a National Party in Multiparty Democracy of Nepal.
6. Both Maoist and Seven Parties accepted their past mistakes and assured to amend them.
7. Both Maoist and Seven Parties were convinced of fighting for the fundamental aspects of Human Rights and ensuring peace and Stability with Freedom.
8. They planned on boycotting the Election declared by King Gyanendra and launching a Peaceful People's Movement.
9. They requested Diplomatic and Moral Support from the International Community.

Comprehensive Peace Accord

Introduction

Comprehensive Peace Accord was a Tripartite Agreement signed between The King- King Gyanendra, The Maoist- Pushpa Kamal Dahal and Representative of Paties- Girija Prasad Koirala on Mangsir 6th 2063 B.S.

Features of Comprehensive Peace Accord

- The Maoist People's Army was to be provided temporary barracks, where they would be rehabilitated.
- Both armies to be monitored and supervised by the United Nations Mission in Nepal, as per the earlier agreement reached between the government and the Maoists.

- Strict implementation of all previous pacts/agreements reached between the government and Maoists.
- Termination of the military action and the armed mobilization. Both sides to stop attacks or any kind of violent and offensive activities from either side; no new recruitment in armed forces of both sides and no transportation of arms and ammunition and explosives.
- Both sides to assist each other to maintain law, peace, and order
- Both sides to fully commit themselves to uphold all international human rights laws and civil liberties, and the Office of the United Nations High Commissioner for Human Rights to monitor the human rights situation.
- The King to be stripped of political rights and his property to be nationalized under public trusts.
- Scrapping of the Maoists' parallel administration (People's governments, People's Courts) across the country.
- Strong punitive policy to curb corruption and confiscation of property earned illegally through corruption
- Formation of National Peace and Rehabilitation Commission, Truth Commission, and a high-level Commission for State Restructuring.
- Respectful rehabilitation and social integration of the people displaced during the insurgency
- Other Features Include Nationalization of All Property, Guarantee Social Security and Labor Rights, Secularism, and provision of other Fundamental Rights

If you have any queries or confusions, email me at studysocialsciencesweb@gmail.com.